An Annotated
Critical Bibliography of
Alfred, Lord Tennyson

An Annotated Critical Bibliography of Alfred, Lord Tennyson

Marion Shaw

with the assistance of Clifton U. Snaith

HARVESTER WHEATSHEAF

ST. MARTIN'S PRESS

First published 1989 by
Harvester Wheatsheaf,
66 Wood Lane End, Hemel Hempstead,
Hertfordshire, HP2 4RG
A division of
Simon & Schuster International Group

and in the USA by
St. Martin's Press Inc.
175 Fifth Avenue, New York, NY 10010

Printed and bound in Great Britain by
Billing and Sons Ltd, Worcester.

Library of Congress Cataloging-in-Publication Data

Shaw, Marion
An annotated critical bibliography of Alfred, Lord Tennyson /
Marion Shaw, with the assistance of Clifton U. Snaith.
p.   cm.
Includes index.
ISBN 0-312-01962-9
1.Tennyson, Alfred Tennyson, Baron, 1809–1892 – Bibliography
I. Snaith, Clifton U.   II. Title
Z8866.S52   1989
(PR5581)
018.821'8–dc20   89-35427
CIP

British Library Cataloguing in Publication Data

Shaw, Marion
An annotated critical bibliography of Alfred Lord
Tennyson. (Harvester annotated critical bibliographies).
1. Poetry in English. Tennyson, Alfred, Baron,
1809–1898. Bibliographies
I. Title
016.821'8

ISBN 0-7108-0969-7

---

1 2 3 4 5   93 92 91 90 89

Contents

Acknowledgements

I wish to acknowledge with gratitude the courteous and efficient help given to me during the preparation of this bibliography by the librarians and staff of the Brynmor Jones Library, the University of Hull. I also wish to record my thanks to the librarians at the Tennyson Research Centre, Lincoln, particularly Sue Gates.

Advice to the Reader

This is an annotated, selected bibliography of works on Tennyson which I have divided into three main sections: biography; bibliography and related matters; and criticism. Within these sections there are subdivisions so that any reader wishing to scan what criticism there is on, for example, *In Memoriam*, or to gain an overview of the position with regard to the manuscripts of Tennyson's poems, may do so conveniently. There is also a short section, a kind of coda, on Tennyson's plays which, since so little has been written about them, is not subdivided.

The entries have been arranged in the chronological order of their publication with the intention, common to the *Harvester Annotated Critical Bibliographies*, of showing the development of attitudes to Tennyson's work and life, and the general evolution of Tennyson studies. An exception to this pattern is the placing of Tennyson's own letters at the beginning of that particular subsection, even though they were not first published until 1980 and are still in progress. As the only prose that Tennyson wrote, it seems right to give them this kind of precedence. Similarly, *The Tennyson Archive* (70), which reproduces in facsimile almost all of Tennyson's poetic manuscripts, has been placed at the beginning of the section on manuscripts and manuscript studies.

Each subsection on an individual poem, or on a group of poems, is prefaced with a brief account of the publication of the poem or poems and of any circumstances connected with the publication which seem to be of interest, such as the origins of *Maud* in a lyric written more than twenty years earlier. In this kind of information, as in all matters pertaining to the study of Tennyson's poetry, I am deeply indebted to Christopher Ricks's great edition of *The Poems of Tennyson* (92).

Some cross-referencing has been included. This particularly relates to articles which appear in collections of essays; the article is discussed in its relevant section and listed in the collection, with cross-references made to the separate entries.

In preparing a bibliography of this kind, the question arises: Who is it for? I think the persons who have most been in my mind as requiring a book of this kind are the keen undergraduate, the postgraduate student beginning work on Tennyson, and the teacher at school, university or college who wants to take bearings in the biographical and critical field. This bibliography has not been written with

Tennyson experts primarily in mind because they will already have been over the territory themselves.

As a selection this book is inevitably partial, representing my choice of what is essential or good or useful or, very occasionally, to be avoided. Sometimes items have been included because there is nothing else, or very little else, on the work in question. Tennyson's plays are in this category; there is a great lack of criticism of them. As Henry James pointed out, they aren't Tennysonian; nevertheless they represent Tennyson's heartfelt wish, common to many Victorian writers, to approach an audience directly, face to face, and they are interesting in this respect as well as in their preoccupation with the themes of national identity and the responsibilities of leadership.

Introduction

Kirk H. Beetz's bibliography of Tennyson (113), which is the most complete listing of writings about him to 1982, has more than 5,000 items. Although this includes dissertation abstracts and reviews, it still represents a formidable amount of published material. And there is no reason to believe that the annual output of books and articles on Tennyson will decrease: rather the reverse. Tennyson would have been flattered and gratified and at the same time terrified and appalled. One of his greatest fears was that his poetry would not last, yet he did not want to be remembered to suffer 'the irreverent doom / Of those that wear the Poet's crown . . . [When] round him ere he scarce be cold / Begins the scandal and the cry'.

Tennyson's sensitivity to criticism was exercised from the time of his earliest publications. The admiration of his very first critics, particularly Arthur Hallam, and Hallam's recognition of 'sensational' and Romantic qualities in Tennyson's verse, roused the wrath of the Tory reviewers and resulted in Croker's hostilities in the *Quarterly Review* (221). So began a divided and contentious response to Tennyson's poetry which, with variations, has continued almost unabated ever since and is different from the kind of reception given to other poets – Arnold or Yeats, for example. Critics have always seemed to be either for Tennyson or against him to quite extreme degrees, and the opposing arguments have led not only to liveliness of debate on Tennyson's poetry in particular but also on the nature of poetry in general. The history of Tennyson criticism provides a sharp focus on the aesthetic questions which have occupied both poets and critics for the last century and a half.

Arthur Hallam's review (220) divided poets into those who feel and those who think. Hallam attributed to the former category, to which Tennyson belonged, a Romantic sensibility exquisitely and spontaneously responsive to stimuli, and to the latter category a reflective and proselytising cast of mind which was more prosaic, less true to the essential character of a poet. The ideally great poet was born into the first category and cultivated the qualities of the second, and this was a compromise recommended by John Stuart Mill (222) who, following Hallam, found Tennyson to be constitutionally a poet of heightened sensibilities in whom the moral and educative purposes of the reflective poet should be inculcated.

Both Hallam and Mill made the distinction between the types of poet with some subtlety, but later Victorian critics tended to make a reductive equation of the two voices of poetry with mere escapism and lyric indulgence on the one hand and seriousness of purpose and social usefulness on the other. During the early years of Tennyson's career, the general opinion was that he was irresponsibly luxurious and fanciful; John Sterling's review (223) of the 1842 volumes of *Poems*, for instance, or J. W. Marston's of *The Princess* (225) were highly cautionary on the grounds of Tennyson's apparent refusal to take his poet's mission seriously and his propensity to indulge in sensuous evocations and medieval fantasies. This response to *The Princess* is surprising in that in its concern with the higher education of women it represented Tennyson's attempt to tackle one of the 'two great social questions impending in England' (the other being 'the housing and education of the poor man before making him our master') (*Memoir* I 249). The fairy-tale narrative of the poem, and its chivalric trappings, were obviously only too successful as a disguise for its topical concerns.

With *In Memoriam*, however, accusations of social irrelevance were largely silenced. I have included in this bibliography no contemporary reviews of *In Memoriam* because there was a consensus of critical opinion that Tennyson had discovered an appropriate blend of the personal and the public, the thoughtful and the luxurious. The reviews were concerned to praise and quote the poem, to recommend both its homely appeal and its honourable status within the English and Classical elegiac tradition. With *In Memoriam* there was a critical quietus and Tennyson enjoyed an unprecedented sense of having become the poet of the age.

But with *Maud* the disputes revived. As the reviews by Aytoun (316) and Gladstone (318) make clear, Tennyson's most strenuous effort to date to write a socially conscious poem was seen as poetically indecorous: 'unhappy, unwholesome, and disagreeable', Aytoun called it, and Gladstone thought it tangled in political matters beyond the competence of its author. But the volume sold well – 8,000 copies in three months – and Tennyson bought Farringford with the proceeds. This financial success was compounded by the sales of *Idylls of the King* in 1859 and *Enoch Arden and Other Poems* in 1864, which sold more than 40,000 copies in the first year. This was the high tide not only of Tennyson's popularity but also of his critical reputation. For the period of a little more than a decade, from *In Memoriam* to *Enoch Arden*, and allowing for the fall from grace that *Maud* occasioned, there was a homogeneity of critical opinion concerning his greatness and his suitability to the age; what arguments there were – in *The Times*, for instance – were concerned with whether or not he was a genius of the stature of Milton.

Towards the end of this reign, however, the serious detraction of Tennyson, which rehearsed the old dichotomies but did so with more measured consideration and with an overview of his maturing career, was under way, and its marker is Bagehot's brilliantly destructive review of *Enoch Arden and Other Poems* (203). Bagehot, and in a slightly different way Swinburne too (346), are objecting to Tennyson on the double score of banality of conception *and* a disproportionately decorative style. The opposition that Hallam and Mill had advanced between the sensuous and the philosophical qualities of poetry now seems to have become a double liability as far as Tennyson's critical reputation is concerned; he is too much the poet of the Victorian age, too careful of its morality and attuned to its sensibilities, and consequently the brilliance of his style has the appearance of a euphemism.

In 1917, when A. C. Bradley (151) wrote his summary of Tennyson's position, he was reflecting on a pattern of late Victorian and early twentieth-century criticism in which a genuine reaction to Tennyson was compounded by a virulent anti-Victorianism fuelling hostility against its most representative poet. Bradley was writing amid the Modernist revolt against the previous age, as in Yeats (142), and during a war which many – Fausset, for example (118) – had come almost to believe was Tennyson's fault, or at least the fault of the Victorian commercialism and complacency of which Tennyson seemed to be the spokesman.

This is the background to Harold Nicolson's famous book on Tennyson (7), published in 1923, which took both an old and a new view of his poetry. It was old in that, like the early Victorian critics, it said there were two Tennysons, the dreamy mystic and the responsible bard. But in Nicolson's case, and in this he sets the note of much future twentieth-century criticism, it is the brooding, melancholy Tennyson who is preferred. What was also new about Nicolson was the way in which he brought Tennyson unmistakably into the twentieth century. However partial his estimate of Tennyson, and coloured by a Bloomsbury-like distaste for the utilitarian and popular in poetry, Nicolson treats Tennyson as a fascinating psychological case worthy of serious investigation; in this respect Nicolson makes Tennyson a modern, indeed a Freudian, figure and rescues him from historical fustiness. By contrast, Leavis's strictures (138) seem old-fashioned, spreading from the heart of Victorian moralism itself.

Of the period before and during the Second World War, there seems to have been a post-Nicolson begrudging concentration of attention on the impressionistic and melancholy side of Tennyson. To a New Critic like Brooks (229) Tennyson's acknowledged greatness is in spite of himself, and this accords with Auden's view (88) that Tennyson was really very stupid but somehow, unconsciously almost, he wrote mellifluous and resonant poetry about despair.

Nevertheless, within the two-voices critical field that Nicolson had established there began to be powerful rehabilitations: E. D. H. Johnson (140) believed Tennyson to have been a maimed poet but this did not stop Johnson from believing that what Tennyson did well, he did very well indeed. Arthur J. Carr's brilliant essay (139) likewise takes a tragic view of Tennyson's career, but Carr is a critic whose admiration for Tennyson's excellences is unembarrassed and passionate, and in some respects this essay, written in 1950, can be seen as the sign of the tide having turned yet again. It is with Jerome H. Buckley's *Tennyson* (121), and with John Killham's collection of essays (122), both of them published in 1960, that there is an acknowledgement of Tennyson as a totality and not as a figure of shattered and fragmented genius.

Tennyson's reputation as a weighty and serious poet, who could rank with Wordsworth, for example, was also given substance in 1960 by the foundation of the Tennyson Society. This was due to the efforts of the poet's grandson Charles Tennyson who, since the death of his uncle, Hallam Tennyson, in 1928 had been working on Tennyson's unpublished poems and on a biography to supplement the highly respectful and discreet *Memoir* (3). Charles Tennyson's biography (8), which humanised Tennyson and revealed much about the legendary 'black-bloodedness' of the Tennyson family, was published in 1949 and this too helped to contribute to the sense of Tennyson's modernity. The foundation of the Tennyson Society led to the establishment of the Tennyson Research Centre in Lincoln in 1964, which has now become an important resource library for students of Tennyson (107). In 1967, under the guidance of the then Secretary, R. F. Smith, the Tennyson Society began to publish the *Tennyson Research Bulletin*, which is issued to members (now more than 500) annually. No student of Tennyson should ignore the *Tennyson Research Bulletin*, which not only carries major biographical and critical articles but also contains numerous small items of interest, including reviews, which only an author-journal of this type can supply.

During the last twenty years Tennyson scholarship has been inestimably aided by Christopher Ricks's edition of *The Poems of Tennyson* (92). This has not only helped critics to be more aware of Tennyson's compositional methods and the facts surrounding the publication of his poems, but its influence also seems to have fostered seriousness and intensity in critical studies. Books like Alan Sinfield's *The Language of Tennyson's In Memoriam* (293), F. E. L. Priestley's *Language and Structure in Tennyson's Poetry* (211), W. David Shaw's *Tennyson's Style* (214) and Paul Turner's *Tennyson* (126), all dating from the 1970s, seem to possess a new rigour and professionalism in their approach to Tennyson.

Recent criticism has also shown an increased interest in *Idylls of the King*. For so long regarded as a falling-off of Tennyson's powers, *Idylls* now seems to be the most written about of Tennyson's long poems, with Rosenberg (374) providing one of the earlier, and probably the best, of several full-length studies of the poem. Elliot L. Gilbert's essay on 'The Female King' (385) demonstrates Tennyson's growing exposure to psychoanalytic, feminist and post-structuralist readings.

Although more slowly than Browning, Tennyson is coming to be regarded as a 'modern' poet in the sense of one whose poetry can be excitingly deconstructed. Yet even in this there is the shadow of a circle once more becoming fully rounded; when T. S. Eliot wrote in 1936 that in *Maud*, in Tennyson in general, there is 'emotion so deeply suppressed, even from himself . . . . emotion which . . attained no ultimate purgation' (278), he was forecasting a version of the 'two-voices' complaint which would uncannily surface in modern criticism – in, for instance, Alan Sinfield's comment about Tennyson (135), made in 1986, that 'his writing is not the representation of a unified self'. This is not so very different from Nicolson's 'unhappy mystic of the Lincolnshire wolds' or, for that matter, from the opinion of Arthur Hallam, who still remains one of Tennyson's finest critics, that Tennyson belonged to that group of poets whose physical constitution was so exquisitely tuned that it forced them into a kind of dissociated sensibility, a state of feeling split off from the common experience of 'duller temperaments'. Hallam and Sinfield may approach Tennyson's poetry from different philosophical and political positions but their criticism of it shares a common sense of its darkly troubled and dissembling surfaces.

Chronological Table of Tennyson's Life and Chief Publications

1809   (6 August) Alfred Tennyson born at Somersby, Lincolnshire, fourth child (of an eventual eleven children) of Revd George Clayton Tennyson, Rector of Somersby, and Elizabeth (Fytche) Tennyson. T's childhood and youth were embittered by family feuds (his father was disinherited) and by his father's drunkenness and mental instability.

1816–20   Attended Louth Grammar School, which he hated. Subsequently educated at home by his father.

1827   *Poems by Two Brothers* (with elder brothers Frederick and Charles).
Entered Trinity College, Cambridge.

1829   Met Arthur Henry Hallam, also a student at Trinity College, who was to become T's close friend and the fiancé of his sister, Emily.
T became a member of the 'Apostles', a Cambridge debating society, to which Hallam also belonged: a relatively happy time.

1830   *Poems, Chiefly Lyrical*.

1831   Death of T's father; T left Cambridge without taking a degree.

1832   *Poems* (harshly criticised in *Quarterly Review*).

1833   Death of Hallam from cerebral haemorrhage while on holiday in Vienna.

1834–6   In love with and then disillusioned by Rosa Baring, daughter of a wealthy neighbour.

1837   T's family left Somersby. T engaged to Emily Sellwood.

1840   Engagement to Emily broken off: beginning of several years of depression, ill health and financial insecurity.

1842   *Poems* (2 vols.: vol. I revisions of previous poems, vol. II new poems).

1847   *The Princess*.

1849   Renewed relationship with Emily Sellwood.

1850	*In Memoriam.* Married Emily Sellwood. Appointed Poet Laureate.
1852	Son Hallam born (followed by Lionel in 1854).
1853	Permanent home at Farringford, Isle of Wight (second home, Aldworth on Surrey/Sussex border, built in 1868).
1855	*Maud and Other Poems.*
1859	*Idylls of the King* (i.e. 'Enid', 'Vivien', 'Elaine' and 'Guinevere'): final sequence completed 1885 with the addition of 'Balin and Balan'.
1864	*Enoch Arden, etc.*
1875	*Queen Mary*, the first of seven plays.
1879	Published *The Lover's Tale* (written *c.* 1830).
1883	Accepted the offer of a barony.
1886	Death of his son Lionel.
1889	*Demeter and Other Poems.*
1892	(6 October) T died. (28 October) Posthumous publication of *The Death of Oenone, Akbar's Dream, and Other Poems.*

Abbreviations

BIS	*Browning Institute Studies*
CUP	Cambridge University Press
EC	*Essays in Criticism*
ELH	*Journal of English Literary History*
HSL	*Harvard Studies in Literature*
HUP	Harvard University Press
JEGP	*Journal of English and Germanic Philology*
JPRS	*Journal of Pre-Raphaelite Studies*
MLQ	*Modern Language Quarterly*
NQ	*Notes and Queries*
OUP	Oxford University Press
PMLA	*Publications of the Modern Language Association of America*
PQ	*Philological Quarterly*
RES	*Review of English Studies*
SB	*Studies in Bibliography*
T	Tennyson
TLS	*Times Literary Supplement*
TRB	*Tennyson Research Bulletin*
TRC	Tennyson Research Centre
TSLL	*Texas Studies in Literature and Language*
TSM	*Tennyson Society Monograph*
TSOP	*Tennyson Society Occasional Papers*
UP	University Press
UTQ	*University of Toronto Quarterly*
VN	*Victorian Newsletter*
VP	*Victorian Poetry*
VQR	*Virginia Quarterly Review*
VS	*Victorian Studies*

Biography

Biographies and biographical accounts

1   Ritchie, Anne Thackeray
RECORDS OF TENNYSON, RUSKIN AND ROBERT
AND ELIZABETH BROWNING (New York: Harper &
Bros., 1892)

The section on T was originally written for *Harper's Magazine* in 1883 at T's prompting. It is a personal, impressionistic account by Anne Thackeray, the novelist's daughter, who first met T when she was a child in the 1840s, then grew to know him at Freshwater after her father's death in 1863, and remained his friend to the end of his life. In 1877 she wrote *From the Island*, a novella based on the literary society of Freshwater. See also Hester Ritchie (ed.), *The Letters of Anne Thackeray Ritchie* (London: John Murray, 1924) and Winifred Gérin, *Anne Thackeray Ritchie: A Biography* (Oxford: OUP, 1981).

2   Knowles, James
'Aspects of Tennyson, II: A Personal Reminiscence',
NINETEENTH CENTURY vol. XXXIII (1893) 164–88

By the editor of *Nineteenth Century*, who was also T's friend and the architect of his house, Aldworth, this is an affectionate and admiring account of T as unmusical, sensitive to criticism, spiritually anxious, simple, and straightforward to the point of brusqueness. It contains many anecdotes, an account of the publication of *Poems by Two Brothers*, an early prose version of 'Balin and Balan' and what T told Knowles of the scheme for *Idylls of the King*. It was one of the six commemorative articles in this volume of *Nineteenth Century* in the year after T's death, the others being by Swinburne, Agnes Lambert, Herbert Paul and two by Theodore Watts. (See also 62.)

3   [Tennyson, Hallam, Lord]
     ALFRED LORD TENNYSON: A MEMOIR BY HIS SON,
     2 vols. (London: Macmillan, 1898)

An essential source: although it suppressed much material and is over-respectful and sometimes misleading, it is nevertheless a comprehensive, vital portrait of T by one who was his secretary and amanuensis as well as his son. It contains many comments and unpublished writings by T, letters to and from him, and accounts of his activities and opinions. All subsequent biographies and much criticism begin here. It should be read in conjunction with the biographies by Sir Charles Tennyson (8) and R. B. Martin (24). For an account of the writing of *Memoir* and its predecessor, the privately printed *Materials for a Life of A. T.*, see Elliott (19).

4   Allingham, H. and Radford, D. (eds.)
     WILLIAM ALLINGHAM, A DIARY (London: Macmillan, 1907; London and Sussex: Centaur Press, 1967, with an introduction by Geoffrey Grigson)

Allingham was T's Boswell and his *Diary*, kept from 1824 until his death in 1889, is indispensable biographical reading. A customs officer, a minor poet, a lover of literature and literary London, an engagingly modest yet intrusive man, Allingham made his way into the 'much-longed-for-presence' of T in 1851. His *Diary* records his meetings with T (and with other literary notables) in vivid detail:

> Wednesday, April 3 [1867] – Farringford. Tennyson and I busied ourselves in the shrubberies, transplanting primroses with spade, knife, and wheelbarrow. After dinner T. concocts an experimental punch with whisky and claret – not successful. Talk of Publishers, anon of higher things. He said, 'I feel myself to be a centre – can't believe I shall die. Sometimes I have doubts of a morning' . . . We spoke of Swedenborg, animals, etc., all with the friendliest sympathy and mutual understanding. T. is the most delightful man in the world to converse with, even when he disagrees.

5   Tennyson, Hallam, Lord (ed.)
     TENNYSON AND HIS FRIENDS (London: Macmillan, 1911)

Reminiscences of T by his family and friends gathered together by his son as a 'sequel' to the *Memoir* and including T's poems about his friends. The contributors include T's wife Emily, friends or the children of friends, such as Edward FitzGerald, James Knowles and William Rawnsley, and scientists, divines and savants who knew T and his work towards the latter part of his life. The attitudes are reverential, as was to be expected under Hallam's editorial care, but the volume is valuable in its comprehensiveness and for its many reported conversations and its depiction of the social groupings T knew at various stages in his life.

6   Lounsbury, Thomas R.
THE LIFE AND TIMES OF TENNYSON (London: OUP;
New Haven: Yale UP, 1915)

Leisurely and capacious, although unfinished (it covers the period of T's life to 1850) account of T's life and poetry in relation to his contemporary literary scene. Particularly useful on the critical opinions of the time, on T's reputation and on the power of periodical reviewing, although some of the information, specifically Lounsbury's attribution to Lockhart of the hostile review in the *Quarterly* of T's *Poems* (1832), has been shown to be inaccurate. Nevertheless, Lounsbury's is the first worthwhile attempt to contextualise T's life and poetry, and his critical insights are still valuable.

7   Nicolson, Harold
TENNYSON: ASPECTS OF HIS LIFE, CHARACTER
AND POETRY (London: Constable, 1923)

Still one of the most readable and provocative studies, this brilliantly written and influential, although condescending and partial, rescue of T from early-twentieth-century critical derision and dislike involved Nicolson in detaching T from the Victorian age. In Nicolson's opinion, the 'unfortunate condition of contemporary literary taste' forced T into 'a perpetual straining after objective expression' which inhibited the true subjective nature of his talent. In his claim that the 'real' T was 'not a Victorian at all but a later Georgian', Nicolson rejected most of T's Laureate poetry and recommended those poems which he believed came from T's 'essential inspiration of fear':

'Ulysses', 'The Lotos-Eaters', 'Tithonus', *Maud*, and, 'after all, *In Memoriam*'. Nicolson's division of T into 'an extremely good emotional poet [and] a second-rate instructional bard' was a powerful proponent of the 'two-voices' critical debate concerning T.

8   Tennyson, Charles
ALFRED TENNYSON: By his grandson (London: Macmillan, 1949; reissued with alterations, 1968)

For many years the standard biography: Charles Tennyson used private papers and his own memories to give an honest, sympathetic but clear-sighted account, telling the truth for the first time about the unhappiness of T's childhood. It is informed by judicious admiration for the poetry and provides a corrective to the hagiography of Hallam Tennyson's *Memoir* without losing respect and affection for T as a man.

9   Abell, Arthur, M. (ed.)
CONVERSATIONS WITH GREAT COMPOSERS (London: Spiritualist Press [1957])

This records a conversation between Brahms, Joachim and T which took place just before T's death (although T had known Joachim for many years) in which T expressed belief in evolution as only the 'outer shell' and nature as the servant of God, and in the separateness of the individual soul and the preservation of form beyond death.

10   Richardson, Joanna
THE PRE-EMINENT VICTORIAN. A STUDY OF TENNYSON (London: Jonathan Cape, 1962)

T as a 'Victorian husband and father, a Victorian philosopher and moralist . . . to his contemporaries, the incarnation of poetry and, indeed, of their own higher thinking'. Not a 'portrait of an age' but an affectionate and readable account, making (unscholarly) use of letters from family and friends, of T's domestic and social activities.

11   Rader, Ralph Wilson
TENNYSON'S *MAUD*: THE BIOGRAPHICAL GENESIS

(Berkeley: University of California Press (*Perspectives in Criticism* 15), 1963)

Critical detective work which makes enthralling reading on T's relationship with three women – Rosa Baring, Sophie Rawnsley and Emily Sellwood – and the lingering presence of these women in his poetry, particularly *Maud*.

12   Wicks, D. G. B.
'Tennyson in Portugal', *TRB* (1968) paper 3

T went to Portugal in 1859 with F. T. Palgrave. This article draws on Palgrave's account to augment what Hallam included in *Materials* and *Memoir*.

13   Tennyson, Sir Charles
'Alfred Tennyson and Somersby' (Lincoln: The Tennyson Society, 1974)

A description of the family home where T lived from his birth until his family was obliged to vacate it in 1837. Conditions were very cramped, 'sleeping five or six in a room', according to T's father.

14   Hixson, Jerome C.
'Cauteretz Revisited', *TRB* (1975) 145–9

This describes T's three visits to the valley of Cauteretz: in 1830 with Arthur Hallam, in 1861 with his family and in 1874 alone. The first two visits occasioned the poem 'In the Valley of Cauteretz' of which T said, 'Altogether I like the little piece as well as anything I have written' (*Memoir* I 474–5).

15   Tennyson, Sir Charles
'Farringford, Home of Alfred Lord Tennyson' (Lincoln: The Tennyson Society, 1976)

T rented Farringford House in Freshwater, Isle of Wight, in 1853 and bought it in 1856 after the commercial success of *Maud and Other Poems*. Sir Charles describes the house that was T's home for thirty-six years, the alterations he made to it, its daily routine and the visitors he received there.

16   Tennyson, Sir Charles
       'Aldworth, Summer Home of Alfred Lord Tennyson'
       (Lincoln: The Tennyson Society, 1977)

       After the publication of his most popular volume, *Enoch
       Arden, etc.*, T could afford to build a second home in secluded
       Blackdown, near Haslemere on the Surrey/Sussex border, so
       that he could escape the summer tourists in the Isle of Wight.
       Sir Charles describes this splendid Georgian–Gothic house, T's
       Camelot, where he quietly spent much of his time in his later
       years and where he died.

17   Stevenson, Catherine B.
       'Tennyson on Women's Rights'. *TRB* (1977) 23–5

       This makes use of a notebook Hallam Tennyson kept while at
       Marlborough school (1866–72) in which he recorded T's opin-
       ions on the 'woman question'.

18   Scott, Patrick
       'The Cloughs Visit the Tennysons, 1861'. *TRB* (1977) 10–13

       Mrs Clough made notes of the visit during which T was voluble
       on the *Essays and Reviews* debate and also subjected his visitors
       to the 'debauch' of a three-hour reading of *Maud*. See also P. G.
       Scott, 'Tennyson and Clough', *TRB* (1969) 64–70.

19   Elliott, Philip L.
       THE MAKING OF THE *MEMOIR* (Greenville, S.
       Carolina: Furman UP, 1978)

       This is a study of the genesis and development of Hallam
       Tennyson's *Memoir* of his father through six stages from an ur-
       manuscript written and compiled soon after T's death; to *MS
       Materials* (?1894) (in TRC), a ten-volume compilation of text,
       transcribed by Hallam's wife Audrey, plus letters, newspaper
       clippings, and cuttings from books, pamphlets and magazines;
       to the privately printed *Materials for a Life of A. T. Collected
       For My Children*, 4 vols. [1895–6]; to *Tennyson and His Friends*
       (1896; not to be confused with the 1911 publication with the
       same title); to the *Memoir* published in 1897. See also this
       author's 'Materials for a Life of A. T.', *NQ* 28 (October 1981)

415–18, which describes the circumstances of the publication of *Materials* and lists the locations of all copies the author has been able to find.

20   Lozynsky, Artem and Reed, John R. (eds.)
      'A Whitman Disciple Visits Tennyson: An Interview
      Describing Dr. Richard Maurice Bucke's Visit of 9 August
      1891 at Aldworth', *TSM* No. 8 (Lincoln: The Tennyson
      Society, 1977)

The visit of Dr Bucke to T was recorded in September 1891 in an 'interview' between Bucke and Horace Traubel, transcribed by the latter, and in letters from Bucke to Whitman and Traubel. The material confirms other accounts of T in the last years of his life.

21   Colley, Ann C.
      'Alfred Tennyson's "Four Crises": Another View of the
      Water Cure', *TRB* (1978) 64–8

Discusses the severe regimen of the Priessnitz hydrapathic treatment T underwent at Cheltenham in 1843–4 in which the 'crises' were eruptions of boils believed useful in expelling poisons from the system.

22   Hill, Sir Francis
      'The Disinheritance Tradition Reconsidered', *TRB* (1978)
      41–54

In the author's words, this is 'a cold-blooded survey' of T's family's financial relationships, which were not as disadvantageous to the Somersby Tennysons as has been made out.

23   Maxwell, Bennett
      'The Steytler Recordings of Alfred, Lord Tennyson: A
      History', *TRB* (1980) 150–7

An account, which includes the texts on the cylinders and extracts from relevant letters and newspaper reports, of the recording made in 1890 of T reading 'The Charge of the Light Brigade' and other poems. See also Charles Tennyson, 'The

Tennyson Phonograph Records', *Bulletin of the British Institute of Recorded Sound* 3 (Winter 1965) 2–8.

24   Martin, Robert Bernard
      TENNYSON: THE UNQUIET HEART (Oxford: Clarendon Press; London: Faber and Faber, 1980)

This may now be regarded as the standard biography. A full and meticulously documented work which not only collects together what previous biographers have discovered but also adds new information, of which the most interesting and controversial is T's concern with inherited epilepsy. A treasure house of information on T's life but perhaps less than enthusiastic towards his poetry. See Stephen Canham, 'Interview-Review: Robert B. Martin', *Biography: An Interdisciplinary Quarterly* 5 (1982) 74–87, for comments on the writing of this biography. See also Jack Kolb, 'Portraits of Tennyson', *Modern Philology* 81 (1983–4) 173–90, where Kolb takes issue with the use Martin makes of what Kolb considers to be insubstantial evidence, particularly in relation to T's supposed epileptic inheritance. Kolb believes Martin's attribution of T's 'trances' to epileptic seizures is questionable and reductive.

25   Wheatcroft, Andrew
      THE TENNYSON ALBUM. A biography in original photographs with an introduction by Sir John Betjeman (London, Boston and Henley: Routledge & Kegan Paul, 1980)

A pleasant, well-informed and intelligently narrated coffee-table biography of T including numerous pictures of his family, homes and the many eminent Victorians he knew. This book is quite the best of its kind as a general, gentle and enjoyable introduction to T.

26   Ormond, Leonée
      'Tennyson and Thomas Woolner', *TSM* No. 9 (Lincoln: The Tennyson Society, 1981)

Using the unpublished diaries and letters of Thomas Woolner, the Pre-Raphaelite sculptor, this pamphlet presents a careful account of what the author describes as the 'steady cross-traffic between these two artists in different media' and their friendship from 1849, when Woolner first persuaded T to sit for a medallion, to their deaths in 1892 within a day of each other.

27   Hoge, James O. (ed.)
LADY TENNYSON'S JOURNAL (Charlottesville: UP of Virginia, 1981)

An 'epitome Journal' put together by Emily Tennyson to assist Hallam in the preparation of the *Memoir* and drawn from the several journals she kept from the time of her marriage to T in 1850 to the time of her serious illness in 1874. An engaging and informal account of daily life in T's household.

28   Page, Norman (ed.)
TENNYSON: INTERVIEWS AND RECOLLECTIONS
(London: Macmillan, 1983)

A useful selection of extracts from the records and reminiscences of more than forty 'witnesses' of T the man rather than the poet, ranging from the early Lincolnshire days to a description of his funeral, and including famous comments by Carlyle, FitzGerald and Gosse.

29   Collins, Richard
'Recollections of Tennyson by Sir George Prothero in the Tennyson Research Centre', *VN* 66 (Fall 1984) 28–31

Prothero was a historian and editor of *Quarterly Review* who met T during the 1880s. His recollections are interesting for T's reported comments on contemporary literary figures.

30   Waddington, Patrick
'Tennyson and Russia', *TSM* No. 11 (Lincoln: The Tennyson Society, 1987)

An interesting account which demonstrates the impact of events in Russia on T's poetry, especially *Maud*, and supplies new biographical information on his acquaintance with Russian writers, in particular Turgenev.

Letters

31   Lang, Cecil Y. and Shannon, Edgar F. (eds.)
THE LETTERS OF ALFRED LORD TENNYSON.
VOL. I 1821–1850; VOL. II 1851–1870 (Oxford: Clarendon
Press, 1981, 1987)

These are the first two of a projected three volumes of T's
letters and include those written to him as well as by him and
some by his immediate family and close friends. Invaluable in
tracing T's movements and his reactions to events in his life,
such as the birth of his children and the search for a home, they
do not say much about his emotional and intellectual life and
even less about his literary views, which never appeared to go
beyond the kind of comment he made to Coventry Patmore
about a line in *The Angel in the House* as 'hammered up out of
old nail-heads'. This may be because many letters were de-
stroyed after his death by his son so that less than 2,000 now
remain, but a more likely reason is that, as all his friends
complained, T was a reluctant letter-writer – in fact, a reluctant
writer of prose of any kind. As the editors point out, 'Alone
among the major poets, he has left not a single prose essay
written for publication. [He] was first and last a poet, and only a
poet'. The letters in these handsomely presented and informa-
tive volumes reveal a man who was a hypochondriac, essentially
reticent and, as the editors say, 'deft, witty, and *honest*'.

32   Schonfield, Hugh J. (ed.)
LETTERS TO FREDERICK TENNYSON (London:
Hogarth Press, 1930)

Approximately 50 letters, written to T's brother Frederick
between 1830 and 1885. Correspondents include Arthur Hallam, Charles Merivale, R. J. Tennant, Fanny Kemble, the
Brownings and Bulwer Lytton, as well as T, his mother and his
brothers and sisters.

33   Gaskell, Charles Milnes (ed.)
AN ETON BOY, 1820–1830, BEING THE LETTERS OF
J. M. GASKELL FROM ETON AND OXFORD (London:
Constable, 1939)

Gaskell knew Hallam at Eton and his letters record their friendship and also Hallam's growing friendship with T at Cambridge during the period 1829–30.

34 Dyson, Hope and Tennyson, Sir Charles (eds.)
DEAR AND HONOURED LADY: THE
CORRESPONDENCE OF QUEEN VICTORIA AND
ALFRED TENNYSON (London: Macmillan, 1969)

This collection draws on hitherto unpublished material in the Royal Archives at Windsor and TRC. T met Queen Victoria in 1862, the year after Prince Albert's death and the year in which he wrote the 'Dedication', addressed to Albert, to *Idylls of the King*. Although T and the Queen met only six times, their correspondence reveals a mutual and sincere regard and affection.

35 Hoge, James O. (ed.)
THE LETTERS OF EMILY LADY TENNYSON
(University Park and London: Pennsylvania State UP, 1974)

This selection of 382 of Emily Tennyson's letters covers fifty years of her life from shortly before her marriage to a week before her death in 1896. No letters survive from the periods of her early engagement to T and her estrangement from him in the 1840s. Emily emerges as an intelligent and loving wife and mother, an efficient organiser of T's social and domestic life, and a correspondent of unpretentious charm and sincerity.

36 Terhune, A. McK. and A. B. (eds.)
THE LETTERS OF EDWARD FITZGERALD, 4 vols.
(Princeton, New Jersey: Princeton UP, 1980)

This collection contains a number of letters to T and his family from 'dear old Fitz', who was T's most enduring friend and a prolific and endearing letter-writer. The editors include helpful 'Biographical Profiles' of the chief of FitzGerald's correspondents, some of whom were T's friends also. For FitzGerald's relationship with T see R. B. Martin, *With Friends Possessed: A Life of Edward FitzGerald* (London and Boston: Faber and Faber, 1985).

37   Kolb, Jack (ed.)
      THE LETTERS OF ARTHUR HENRY HALLAM
      (Columbus: Ohio State UP, 1981)

A densely annotated collection of all known surviving letters
and fragments by and to Arthur Hallam dating from August
1824 to four days before his death in 1833. No letters from T but
some to him (not included in Lang and Shannon), to T's sister
Emily (Hallam's fiancée), to Hallam's family and to members
of the Apostles. There is an interesting review article on the
edition, 'The Worth of Change: The Arthur Hallam Letters',
by Eric Griffiths in *TRB* (1983) 72–80.

38   Day, Aidan
      'Edward FitzGerald to the Tennysons: Three Letters', *NQ*
      227 (August 1982) 303–7

This publishes three letters in TRC from FitzGerald to Emily
and Hallam written in 1872 after the Tennysons' surprise visit to
FitzGerald in Woodbridge that year. The main matter is
Samuel Laurence's portrait of T. Terhune edition of
FitzGerald's *Letters* omits two of these letters and gives only an
extract from the third.

39   Kolb, Jack
      'Tennyson's Epithalamion: Another Account', *PQ* 64 (1985)
      139–45

Includes a letter from Emily Tennyson (Jesse) to Julia Hallam
describing the wedding of Cecilia Tennyson to Edmund
Lushington, which T celebrates in the 'Epilogue' to *In
Memoriam*.

40   Peters, Robert (ed.)
      LETTERS TO A TUTOR: THE TENNYSON FAMILY
      LETTERS TO HENRY GRAHAM DAKYNS (1861–1911)
      (Metuchen, New Jersey and London: Scarecrow Press, 1988)

'Little Dakyns' was the well-liked tutor to T's sons for ten
months during 1861 and remained in correspondence with the
family until his death. Most of the letters in this volume are

from Hallam Tennyson, none from T himself. They reveal much of interest about T's home life.

Other material of biographical interest

41   [Hallam, Henry (ed.)]
REMAINS IN VERSE AND PROSE OF ARTHUR
HENRY HALLAM (London: John Murray, 1834; reprinted
with some changes, 1863)

Privately printed by his father in 1834 and 100 copies distributed, this represents about one-third of Arthur Hallam's compositions and approximately half of those in his father's possession. It contains a selection of poems, essays (including 'On Sympathy', the essay on Cicero, and 'Theodicaea Novissima', which was added at T's request) and an extract from Hallam's review of T's poems. 'Theodicaea Novissima', which was probably read to the Cambridge Apostles in October 1831, is generally reckoned to have had a profound bearing on T's religious thought, particularly as it is expressed in *In Memoriam*. The question Hallam sets out to answer is 'Can man by searching find out God?'; his conclusion is that human reason alone is inadequate to the task and that it is love – 'by which I mean direct, immediate, absorbing affection for one object, on the ground of similarity perceived, and with a view to more complete union' – which, as the noblest quality of the human mind, establishes a sympathetic, reciprocal relationship with the Divine Nature. 'Theodicaea Novissima' was omitted from *Remains* (1863). See Kolb (37), Motter (44) and Hunt (290).

42   Turner, Charles Tennyson
COLLECTED SONNETS, ed. James Spedding and Hallam
Tennyson (London: Kegan Paul, 1880)

Contains a prefatory poem by T, written to commemorate the death of his favourite brother. For a commentary on this and on Charles's poems, see Roger Evans, 'Tennyson's "Midnight, June 30, 1879" and the Sonnets of Charles Tennyson Turner', *TRB* (1983) 81–91. Charles's poems are also discussed by J. R. Ebbatson, 'The Lonely Garden: The Sonnets of Charles Tennyson Turner', *VP* 15 (1977) 307–19.

43   Brookfield, Charles and Frances
        MRS. BROOKFIELD AND HER CIRCLE, 2 vols.
        (London: Sir Isaac Pitman and Sons, 1905)

        William Henry Brookfield ('old Brooks . . . You man of hu-
        morous-melancholy mark') was at Trinity College with T; his
        wife, Jane (Elton) was Arthur Hallam's cousin. This is an
        account, much of it in letters, of this witty and attractive woman
        and her friends who included Thackeray and the Carlyles as
        well as T.

44   Motter, T. H. Vail (ed.)
        THE WRITINGS OF ARTHUR HALLAM (New York:
        Modern Language Association; London: OUP, 1943)

        Henry Hallam's *Remains in Verse and Prose of Arthur Henry
        Hallam* (1834) suppressed half the prose and nearly two-thirds
        of the verse that Motter here collects together. This essential
        source for students interested in Hallam's influence on T pres-
        ents in chronological order his poems, translations from
        Dante's *Vita Nuova*, prose essays (including 'On Sympathy'
        and 'Theodicaea Novissima') and reviews. A scholarly com-
        mentary gives details of composition and explains references.

45   Pope-Hennessy, James
        MONCKTON MILNES: THE YEARS OF PROMISE.
        1809–1851 (London: Constable, 1949)

        This is the first of a two-volume biography (the other volume
        being *The Flight of Youth, 1851–1885* (1951)) of T's friend
        Monckton Milnes (Lord Houghton) and includes an interesting
        evocation of the life-style of the Apostles, placing T's relation-
        ship with Hallam in the context of 'the almost Elizabethan
        conception of friendship' prevalent at the time.

46   Tennyson, Sir Charles
        STARS AND MARKETS (London: Chatto and Windus,
        1957)

        This is the autobiography of T's grandson and biographer (see
        8), which includes childhood memories of T and also describes
        the management of the literary estate after Hallam's death in
        1928 and the writing of the biography.

47 Tennyson, Sir Charles and Baker, F. T. (eds.)
'Some Unpublished Poems by Arthur Henry Hallam'
(Publications of The Tennyson Society), Supplement to *VP* 3
(1965)

These are thirty-five poems, all but one in a notebook inscribed
'Emily Tennyson. Feby. 18th 1836' in 'Manuscript Volumes of
Arthur Hallam's Poems', No. 344 in the Tennyson Collection,
then in the Usher Gallery, Lincoln, now in TRC, Lincoln. The
poems fall into three groups: 'Somersby Sonnets' (1830–1),
'Sonnets Written after My Return from Somersby May 1830'
(mistakenly dated by Sir Charles and Mr Baker as having been
written at Christmas 1830–1) and poems written 1831–2.

48 Tennyson, Sir Charles
'A Poet's Child: The Early Days of Lionel Tennyson', *TRB*
(1970) 91–8

An account of the happy childhood of T's second son, Lionel,
by his son, Sir Charles Tennyson. A further account is given in
'Lionel Tennyson: A Letter from F. T. Palgrave to Lord
[Hallam] Tennyson', an article prepared for publication in
Nineteenth Century in 1899 but not published. It was discovered
in TRC and published in *TRB* (1972) 15–24.

49 Collins, Philip
'Reading Aloud: A Victorian Metier', *TSM* No. 5 (Lincoln:
The Tennyson Society, 1972)

An enjoyable account which includes descriptions of T's draw-
ing-room performances of *Maud* and other favourite poems.

50 Griffiths, David N.
'Tennyson and Gladstone', *TRB* (1972) 1–5

This brief account of T's slightly tetchy relationship with
Gladstone was given as the Tennyson Memorial Sermon in Bag
Enderby Church on Sunday 6 August 1972. See also Gerhard
Joseph, 'The Homeric Competitions of Tennyson and
Gladstone', *BIS* 10 (1982) 105–15.

51   Woolf, Virginia and Fry, Roger (eds.)
      VICTORIAN PHOTOGRAPHS OF FAMOUS MEN AND
      FAIR WOMEN BY JULIA MARGARET CAMERON
      (London: The Hogarth Press, 1926; expanded and revised by
      Tristram Powell, 1973)

      A delightful volume of photographs by T's remarkable neigh-
      bour on the Isle of Wight, Julia Margaret Cameron, who was
      one of the pioneers of photography and who was Virginia
      Woolf's aunt. The volume contains two photographs of T; one
      of them he called 'the dirty monk'.

52   Jenkins, Elizabeth
      'Tennyson and Dr. Gully', *TSOP* No. 3 (Lincoln: The
      Tennyson Society, 1974)

      Dr Gully and his partner, Dr Wilson, established the Malvern
      water cure in 1834. This pamphlet discusses the career of the
      celebrated doctor whose patient T became in 1847.

53   Tennyson, Sir Charles and Dyson, Hope
      THE TENNYSONS: BACKGROUND TO GENIUS
      (London and Basingstoke: Macmillan, 1974)

      A history of the Tennyson family from its origins in South
      Yorkshire to T's parents, his aunts and uncles, and the 'extraor-
      dinary brood' of his ten brothers and sisters.

54   Hixson, Jerome C. and Scott, Patrick
      'Tennyson's Books', *TRB* (1976) 190–9

      A very useful account of T's extensive and eclectic reading from
      childhood onwards; it draws on the libraries of T's father, his
      brother Charles Tennyson-Turner, and his own collections
      from Farringford and Aldworth, as well as other family hold-
      ings, the bulk of which are housed in TRC in Lincoln and
      catalogued in *Tennyson in Lincoln* I (107).

55   Sait, J. E.
      'Tennyson and Longfellow: Some Letters and a Tea Party',
      TRB (1976) 184–9

56   Edwards, P. B.
        'Tennyson and the Young Person', *VP* 15 (1977) 78–82

        This describes the double standard whereby poets were allowed
        much greater licence than novelists in sexual matters, an in-
        justice that the much censured Rhoda Broughton noted in *Not
        Wisely But Too Well*, whose heroine quotes T extensively.

57   Kolb, Jack
        'Arthur Hallam and Emily Tennyson', *RES* 28 (1977) 32–48

        Assembles the evidence concerning the date of Arthur Hal-
        lam's meeting with T's sister Emily and concludes that it took
        place in April 1830 rather than December 1829 as stated by
        Hallam Tennyson. Kolb also discusses the obstacles to their
        engagement and the flaws in their relationship and doubts that
        'the blissful union envisaged in *In Memoriam* could ever have
        been realized'.

58   Allen, Peter
        THE CAMBRIDGE APOSTLES: THE EARLY YEARS
        (London, New York, Melbourne: Cambridge UP, 1978)

        The Cambridge Conversazione Society, more popularly known
        as the Apostles, was a student society which became 'a training
        ground for a long succession of gifted and unusual men' whose
        ethos was that of 'personal growth through the free interchange
        of opinion'. Allen's concern is with the origins and early history
        of this society, to which T belonged for a few months from
        October 1829. More interesting on the involvement of F. D.
        Maurice and Arthur Hallam than on T, whose membership was
        brief and active participation slight; but this is a useful study for
        an understanding of the intellectual background of T's youth.

59   Shatto, Susan
        'Tennyson's Library', BOOK COLLECTOR 27 (1978)
        494–513

        Drawing on the remains of T's library, now at TRC, this
        summarises the main areas in which T acquired books, and
        outlines the shifts in taste in his reading habits and book
        collecting over a lifetime.

60   Noakes, Vivien
       EDWARD LEAR (Glasgow: Collins, 1968; revised Collins/
       Fontana, 1979)

       A good biography of Lear with many references to T and his
       family, whom Lear met in 1857. T's wife Emily, in particular,
       was sympathetic towards the lonely Lear. (For his illustrations
       of T's poems, see 69.)

61   Hagen, June Steffensen
       TENNYSON AND HIS PUBLISHERS (London:
       Macmillan, 1979)

       Although this brings together much interesting new material,
       most of it in TRC, it uses it in a chatty, anecdotal manner which
       does not do justice to the complexity of the topic. Hagen tries to
       do too many things – biography, criticism, social history – and
       falls short of a serious account of T's relationship with his
       publishers and the impact this had on his writing. For an earlier
       account, see Harold G. Merriam, 'Moxon and Tennyson' in
       Edward Moxon: Publisher of Poets (New York: Columbia UP,
       1939).

62   Metcalf, Priscilla
       JAMES KNOWLES, VICTORIAN EDITOR AND
       ARCHITECT (Oxford: Clarendon Press, 1980)

       Knowles designed Aldworth, T's house on Blackdown; he was
       also a founding member and chief organiser of the Metaphysi-
       cal Society. He was the editor of *Contemporary Review* from
       1870 to 1872 and then editor for more than thirty years of
       Nineteenth Century. A man of tireless energy and varied tal-
       ents, his friendship with T, whom he met in 1866, was carefully
       cultivated and slightly sycophantic but also influential in per-
       suading T to persevere with *Idylls of the King*. This biography
       fascinatingly presents a man who was 'catalyst and reflector –
       and occasional irritant – to a great poet' as well as importantly
       representative of his times. (See also 2.)

63   Ormond, Leonée
      'George Frederick Watts: The Portraits of Tennyson', *TRB*
      (1983) 47–58

      On the several portraits, and the famous unfinished statue now
      outside Lincoln Cathedral, by T's most sympathetic and admir-
      ing portrayer.

64   Knies, Earl A. (ed.)
      TENNYSON AT ALDWORTH. THE DIARY OF JAMES
      HENRY MANGLES (Athens, Ohio and London: Ohio
      State UP, 1984)

      Mangles was T's closest neighbour at Aldworth and from 1870
      to 1872 kept a diary which was recovered in 1961. This lively
      document gives a strong sense of T's personality as well as
      recording his response to current events such as the Franco-
      Prussian War, the Byron controversy and the discovery of Mars
      and Saturn.

65   Weaver, Mike
      JULIA MARGARET CAMERON, 1815–1879 (London:
      The Herbert Press, 1984)

      A vividly interesting book based on an exhibition arranged by
      the John Hansard Gallery, University of Southampton, and
      toured by the Arts Council 1984–5. It includes several photo-
      graphs of T (as well as other Victorian sages) and also of
      tableaux and characters from his poems, particularly *Idylls*. In
      addition, it contains some of Julia Margaret Cameron's
      writings.

66   Waller, John O.
      A CIRCLE OF FRIENDS: THE TENNYSONS AND THE
      LUSHINGTONS OF PARK HOUSE (Columbus: Ohio
      State UP, 1986)

      A full and scrupulously researched biography of Edmund and
      Henry Lushington: one became T's brother-in-law and the
      other was the friend whose criticism of poetry T valued highly
      and to whom he dedicated the second edition of *The Princess*.

67   Kolb, Jack
       'Morte d'Arthur: The Death of Arthur Henry Hallam',
       Biography: An Interdisciplinary Quarterly 9 (1986) 37–58

       Describes in lurid detail the circumstances of Hallam's death,
       his previous symptoms and premonitions of early death, the
       findings of the autopsy, and the 'poetic transformation' of these
       facts in T's several descriptions of the death of Arthur, par-
       ticularly in 'Morte d'Arthur'.

68   Hughes, Linda K.
       'From Parlor to Concert Hall: Arthur Somervell's Song-Cycle
       on Tennyson's *Maud*', *VS* 30 (1986) 113–29

       Somervell's song-cycle was published in 1898 and is a fascinat-
       ing cross-section of Victorian and Modernist elements in music.

69   Pitman, Ruth (ed.)
       EDWARD LEAR'S TENNYSON (Manchester: Carcanet,
       1988)

       This delightful book reproduces a set of 200 wash drawings
       prepared in 1884–5 by Edward Lear to illustrate lines of land-
       scape description from T's poems, particularly *Poems* (1842).
       The set was in TRC but was sold and dispersed in 1980; Ruth
       Pitman was instrumental in recording the set before its
       dispersal.

Bibliography

Manuscripts and manuscript studies

Most of the manuscripts of Tennyson's poems are in collections at Trinity College, Cambridge, and the Houghton Library, Harvard University. There are manuscript items in the Berg Collection in the New York Public Library, in the Huntington Library, California, in the British Museum and in private collections. There is also a manuscript of *In Memoriam*, along with other manuscript material, particularly letters, and a large collection of proofs, in the Tennyson Research Centre, Lincoln. The Commonplace Book of John Heath, one of T's Cambridge friends, is in the Fitzwilliam Museum, Cambridge.

70   Ricks, Christopher and Day, Aidan (eds.)
      THE TENNYSON ARCHIVE, 30 vols. (New York:
      Garland Publishing, 1986–7 (in progress))

For the scholar wishing to study T's creative processes and the evolution of his texts, this thirty-volume set makes available manuscript materials held in libraries in Britain and the United States, including the collections in Trinity College, Cambridge, in the Houghton Library and in TRC, Lincoln. It reproduces in facsimile over 90 per cent of the extant manuscripts of T's poems (not the plays), with the exception of a few holdings not available for reproduction. The holdings of each library are published together, and the order and cataloguing of the library is maintained. Each facsimile page is annotated to give an identifying description of the poem reproduced and the location of the manuscript. The last volume contains a comprehensive index which also constitutes the most complete census yet prepared of T's extant poetical manuscripts. See also Ricks (92), Shatto and Shaw (94), Shatto (95) and Pfordresher (93) for descriptions of manuscripts.

71   Tennyson, Charles
      'Tennyson Papers. II. J. M. Heath's "Commonplace
      Book" ', *Cornhill Magazine* CLIII (April 1936) 426–49

      A description of the Commonplace Book which contains manu-
      script copies of poems by T and his brothers and friends. There
      is also an account of Heath and his family.

72   Tennyson, Charles
      'Tennyson Papers. III. *Idylls of the King*', *Cornhill Magazine*
      CLIII (May 1936) 534–57

      Discusses the early manuscripts of *Idylls* and comments on T's
      methods of composition, particularly his rejection of material.

73   Tennyson, Charles
      'Tennyson Papers. IV. The Making of *The Princess*', *Cornhill
      Magazine* CLIII (June 1936) 672–80

      Discusses T's creative processes as revealed in the extant
      manuscripts of *The Princess*.

74   Donahue, Mary Joan
      'Tennyson's "Hail Briton!" and "Tithon" in the Heath
      Manuscript', *PMLA* 64 (1949) 385–416

      The two poems, written *c.* 1833, are printed here from Heath's
      Commonplace Book with a detailed discussion – particularly
      with regard to 'Tithon', which was published as 'Tithonus' in
      1860 – of the revisions T made to them. Donahue also provides
      an excellent commentary on the political and personal context
      to the poems.

75   Shannon, Edgar F. and Bond, W. H.
      'Literary Manuscripts of Alfred Tennyson in the Harvard
      Collage Library', *Harvard Library Bulletin* X (1956) 254–74

      This describes and indexes the seventy-two notebooks and 275
      folders of loose papers acquired by the Houghton Library,
      Harvard, from Charles Tennyson in 1955.

76   Hartman, Joan E.
     'The Manuscripts of Tennyson's "Gareth and Lynette" ',
     Harvard Library Bulletin XIII (1959) 239–64

     This is a lively discussion of the changes between first and last
     versions of this *Idyll* and also of the alterations T made to his
     source in Malory. The manuscript changes suggest that T had
     problems with dialogue and action and that he was conscious of
     the need to unify the *Idylls* as a whole.

77   Collins, Rowland
     'The Frederick Tennyson Collection', *VS* VII (Christmas
     Supplement 1963) 56–76

     This describes the holdings in the Lilly Library of Indiana
     University of all known surviving manuscripts of the poetry,
     and much memorabilia, of T's oldest brother.

78   Marshall, George O.
     'Tennyson's "Oh! That 'Twere Possible": A Link Between *In
     Memoriam* and *Maud*', *PMLA* 78 (1963) 225–9

     There are two versions of this poem, dated 1833, in Heath's
     Commonplace Book. In an expanded form, it was the first
     poem to be published (in *The Tribute* in 1837) after Hallam's
     death. Marshall discusses the differences and also the sim-
     ilarities between this poem and *In Memoriam* and *Maud*.

79   Ricks, Christopher
     'The Tennyson Manuscripts at Trinity College Cambridge',
     TLS (21 August 1969) 918–22

     This article was written immediately after Trinity College lifted
     the restriction placed on the manuscripts by Hallam Tennyson
     when he gave them to the College in 1924; the restriction
     prevented them from being copied or quoted, although they
     could be perused. Professor Ricks had not been able to quote
     from these manuscripts in his 1969 edition of the poems. In this
     article he points out that the manuscripts contain little in the
     way of new unpublished poems but are nevertheless important
     because they reveal much about T's methods of composition.
     See also Christopher Ricks, 'Tennyson's Methods of Composi-
     tion', *Proceedings of the British Academy*, 1967, 209–30 (143).

80   Shannon, Edgar F.
        'The Publication of Tennyson's "Lucretius" ', *SB* 34 (1981)
        146–86

        The purpose of this article is to 'clarify textual development
        [and] supply significant insights into the poet's personality and
        method of composition and into the human relationships
        among author, publisher, editor, and wife': virtually a variorum
        edition of the poem.

81   Ricks, Christopher
        'Spedding's Annotations of the Trinity MS of *In Memoriam*',
        TRB (1984) 110–13

        These annotations, which until 1983 were under interdiction,
        offer some interest; many, doubtlessly the more personal and
        critical ones, were erased by Hallam Tennyson. For an account
        of Spedding's influence on T, see Charles Tennyson, 'James
        Spedding and Alfred Tennyson', *TRB* (1974) 96–105.

Editions and selections

82   POEMS (London: Edward Moxon, 1857)

        The illustrated edition which included pictures by Maclise,
        Rossetti, Holman Hunt and Millais. For a description see G. S.
        Layard, *Tennyson and His Pre-Raphaelite Illustrators: A Book
        about a Book* (London: Stock, 1894); Richard L. Stein, 'The
        Pre-Raphaelite Tennyson', *VS* 24 (Spring 1981) 279–301; and
        Jack T. Harris, 'The Pre-Raphaelites and the Moxon Ten-
        nyson', *JPRS* 3 (1983) 26–37.

83   THE WORKS OF ALFRED, LORD TENNYSON, POET
        LAUREATE (London: Macmillan (New Collected Edition,
        in 7 vols.), 1884)

        This edition, and the single-volume edition of the same year, is
        worthy of mention because, according to his son, T 'carefully
        revised' (*Memoir* II 310) his poems in preparation for it. It thus
        represents the last edition of poems written to that date to be
        revised by him. It comprises: Vols. 1–2, Early Poems; Vol. 3,
        Idylls of the King; Vol. 4, *The Princess* and *Maud*; Vol. 5,
        'Enoch Arden' and *In Memoriam*; Vol. 6, *Queen Mary* and
        Harold; Vol. 7, *The Lover's Tale*.

84   Collins, John Churton (ed.)
      THE EARLY POEMS OF ALFRED LORD TENNYSON
      (London: Methuen, 1900)

      With its erudite introduction and notes, Collins's edition points
      out the allusive nature of T's poetry; it is concerned with T's
      poems to 1842 for which it offers some variant readings. (For
      T's response to Collins's critical attentions, see 115.)

85   Tennyson, Hallam, Lord (ed.)
      THE WORKS OF TENNYSON ANNOTATED, 9 vols.
      (London: Macmillan, 1907–8)

      This is the Eversley edition, which was carefully prepared by
      T's son with annotations by the poet, supplemented by Hallam.
      The edition is a valuable source (almost the only source) of
      comments by T about his poetry. It is usually taken as the basic
      text for subsequent editions of the poems. The volumes com-
      prise the following:

      Poems I
      Poems II
      Queen Mary & Harold
      Enoch Arden & In Memoriam
      The Princess & Maud
      Idylls of the King
      Ballads & Other Poems
      Demeter & Other Poems [*The Cup, The Promise of May*]
      Becket & Other Plays [*The Falcon, The Foresters*]

86   Tennyson, Hallam, Lord (ed.)
      THE WORKS OF TENNYSON WITH NOTES BY THE
      AUTHOR (London: Macmillan, 1913)

      A one-volume edition based on Eversley with some changes.

87   Tennyson, Charles (ed.)
      THE DEVIL AND THE LADY BY ALFRED
      TENNYSON (London: Macmillan, 1930)

      Hallam Tennyson gave the most complete manuscript of this
      play, written when T was 14, to Trinity College, Cambridge.
      Charles Tennyson possessed an earlier manuscript. In this

edition he printed the Trinity manuscript with some small corrections from the earlier manuscript.

88   Auden, W. H. (ed.)
TENNYSON: AN INTRODUCTION AND SELECTION
(New York: Doubleday, 1944; London: Phoenix House,
1946)

This contains a fascinating and revealing (of Auden as much as T) introduction which includes famous comments: 'he had the finest ear, perhaps, of any English poet; he was also undoubtedly the stupidest'; 'the feelings which his gift revealed . . were almost entirely those of lonely terror and desire for death'; 'his poems deal with human emotions in their most primitive states'. Auden's selection includes Songs and Lyrics, *In Memoriam* and *Maud* but none of the narrative verse of either *The Princess* or *Idylls of the King*.

89   [Warren, T. Herbert (ed.)]
TENNYSON: POEMS AND PLAYS, originally THE
COMPLETE POETICAL WORKS OF TENNYSON
(London: OUP, revised and enlarged by Frederick Page,
1953; reprinted as TENNYSON: POEMS AND PLAYS,
1965)

This is the Oxford Standard Authors edition, which presents the text without notes. The poems are arranged in order of publication rather than (as in Ricks, 92) composition. It reprints some poems T suppressed. It is the only edition, apart from Eversley, to print all the plays along with the poems.

90   Houghton, W. E. and Stange, G. R. (eds.)
'Tennyson', VICTORIAN POETRY AND POETICS
(Boston: Houghton Mifflin, 1959; revised 1968) 3–162

The section on T in this commodious anthology includes *In Memoriam*, three books from *Idylls of the King*, the Dedication and the closing poem 'To the Queen', and some of the late poems. There is a useful summarising introduction on T's life, poetic career and critical reception.

91 Ricks, Christopher (ed.)
ALFRED TENNYSON: POEMS OF 1842 (London and
Glasgow: Collins (Annotated Student Texts Series), 1968)

A useful edition for sixth-formers and undergraduates of the
two-volume *Poems* (1842) which contained some of T's finest
writing. The annotations give details of composition, influences
on the poems, explanations where necessary and some critical
comments. There is also a selection of critical extracts and a
bibliography.

92 Ricks, Christopher (ed.)
THE POEMS OF TENNYSON (Harlow, Essex: Longman,
1969; revised edition, 3 vols., 1987)

In the 'Longman's Annotated English Poets' series, this edition, particularly in its revised three-volume form which makes
use of the previously interdicted Trinity manuscripts, is of
indispensable service to the student of T's poetry. The text is
based on the Eversley edition but also includes manuscript
poems, a selection of manuscript variant readings, poems
published since Eversley, and annotations drawn from the
comments of T himself and of earlier editors. Ricks also points
to allusions in T's poetry to the writings of his predecessors. The
poems are arranged chronologically and a full account of the
known circumstances of the composition of each poem is given.
The plays are excluded with the exception of the youthful *The
Devil and the Lady*.

93 Pfordresher, John (ed.)
A VARIORUM EDITION OF TENNYSON'S *IDYLLS OF
THE KING* (New York and London: Columbia UP, 1973)

The purpose of this edition is to enable the scholar to make 'a
proper and complete study of the development of this major
poem'. The text is based on Eversley; it supplements Ricks,
who did not give the manuscript variants for *Idylls*, in attempting to record every significant variant from every extant manuscript, printer's proof and published edition from the first drafts
of 'Morte d'Arthur' (1833) to Eversley (1908). Strictly speaking
a text with variant readings and not a variorum edition, it does
not include annotations or a commentary.

94   Shatto, Susan and Shaw, Marion (eds.)
      TENNYSON: *IN MEMORIAM* (Oxford: Clarendon Press,
      1982)

      This edition gives all known variant readings from the manu-
      scripts and the editions; it also describes the manuscripts and
      discusses the relationship between them. An introduction asse-
      mbles the evidence on the poem's composition and discusses
      the formal influences on the poem. There is also a commentary
      which collates remarks of previous editors and critics and offers
      new information.

95   Shatto, Susan (ed.)
      TENNYSON'S *MAUD*: A DEFINITIVE EDITION
      (London: Athlone Press, 1986)

      This gives all known variant readings from the manuscripts and
      editions. It provides a history of the composition of the poem
      and, in a substantial appendix, describes the manuscripts and
      printed texts. A commentary is included.

Bibliographies, concordances and guides

96   Luce, Morton
      A HANDBOOK TO THE WORKS OF ALFRED LORD
      TENNYSON (London: Bell, 1895; revised 1914)

      Designed to accompany the single-volume edition of *Works*
      (London: Macmillan) published in 1894; describes and anno-
      tates the poems and makes sensible general comments; the best
      of its kind from the nineteenth century.

97   Wise, Thomas, J.
      A BIBLIOGRAPHY OF THE WRITINGS OF ALFRED,
      LORD TENNYSON, 2 vols. (Dawsons: London, 1908;
      reprinted 1967)

      In spite of the doubt cast by John Carter and Graham Pollard on
      Wise's honesty as a bibliographer (*An Enquiry into the Nature
      of Certain XIX Century Pamphlets*: London: Constable; New
      York: Scribner, 1934), Wise remains one of the great bibliogra-
      phers and this is still the standard bibliography and an indis-

pensible source for the textual scholar – although it should be used with caution because of Wise's inaccuracies and forgeries. (For a list of Wise's forgeries see William B. Todd, 'A Handlist of Thomas J. Wise' in *Thomas J. Wise: Centenary Studies*, ed. W. B. Todd, 1959.) Wise gives (i) Principal Editions of the poems and the plays; (ii) Contributions to Periodical Literature; (iii) Pirated Issues; (iv) Collected Editions; (v) Biography and Criticism; and (vi) Alphabetical List. See also John O. Eidson, 'Tennyson's Part in the Carter-Pollard Enquiry', *TRB* (1977) 33–5.

98   Baker, Arthur E.
A CONCORDANCE TO THE POETICAL AND
DRAMATIC WORKS OF ALFRED LORD TENNYSON
(London: Routledge & Kegan Paul, 1914; reprinted New
York: Barnes and Noble, 1966)

There are over 1,200 pages of placings, covering all words (except for about 250 common ones listed in a prefatory note) in all poems available to date, including poems contained in *Memoir* and 'suppressed' poems 1830–68.

99   Baker, Arthur E.
A TENNYSON DICTIONARY: THE CHARACTERS
AND PLACE-NAMES CONTAINED IN THE POETICAL
AND DRAMATIC WORKS OF THE POET,
ALPHABETICALLY ARRANGED AND DESCRIBED
WITH SYNOPSES OF THE POEMS AND PLAYS
(London: Routledge; New York: Dutton, 1916)

100   Robinson, Edna Moore
TENNYSON'S USE OF THE BIBLE (Baltimore: John
Hopkins UP, 1917; reprinted 1968)

Not exactly a concordance but an attempt to show T's poetic development as seen in the successive stages of his use of the English Bible. Includes the plays.

101   Baker, Arthur E.
CONCORDANCE TO *THE DEVIL AND THE LADY*
(London: Golden Vista Press, 1931)

102   Killham, John
'Introduction: Tennyson, A Review of Modern Criticism',
CRITICAL ESSAYS ON THE POETRY OF TENNYSON
(London: Routledge & Kegan Paul, 1960) 1–21

Of historical as well as intrinsic interest in that it registered and
helped to promote the beginning of a rise in T's critical reputation. Killham surveys criticism from Bagehot's strictures on
'Enoch Arden' through Yeats's anti-Victorianism to the 'ordeal
by biography' of Fausset and Nicolson and the grudging interest
of the New Critics in T's lyric poetry.

103   Marshall, George O.
A TENNYSON HANDBOOK (New York: Twayne
Publishers, 1963)

This considers only the published poems, is occasionally text-
ually unreliable, and is not very helpful in directing the reader
to critical material.

104   Tennyson, Charles and Fall, Christine
ALFRED TENNYSON: AN ANNOTATED
BIBLIOGRAPHY (Athens, Georgia: University of Georgia
Press, 1967)

In fourteen sections: (1) Bibliographical; (2) Arthur Henry
Hallam; (3) Homes and haunts; (4) Religion, philosophy,
ethics; (5) Tennyson and science; (6) Poems not included in the
collected edition; (7) Annotated editions and selections; (8)
Sources; (9) Bibliographies, concordances, handbooks; (10)
Critical and interpretative: general; (11) Critical and interpretative: specific volumes and major poems; (12) Critical and
interpretative: shorter poems; (13) Tennyson and the reviewers; and (14) The dramas. There are errors in this bibliography and it should be used with caution.

105   Johnson, E. D. H.
'Alfred, Lord Tennyson', THE VICTORIAN POETS: A
GUIDE TO RESEARCH, ed. Frederic E. Faverty, 2nd edn
(Cambridge, Mass.: Harvard UP, 1968) 33–80

This very useful essay is divided into nine sections: (i) Manuscript and Other Source Material; (ii) Bibliography; (iii) Editions; (iv) Biography; (v) Reputation; (vi) Influences; (vii) General Studies; (viii) Special Studies; and (ix) Individual Poems. For the period it covers this is the most helpful guide to criticism of T; it not only gives detailed and accurate information on a comprehensive range of material but also comments helpfully on the fashions and trends in critical responses to T's poetry.

106   Paden, W. D. and Lawrence, Dan H.
'Alfred, 1st Baron Tennyson', NEW CAMBRIDGE BIBLIOGRAPHY OF ENGLISH LITERATURE, vol. III 1800–1900, ed. George Watson (Cambridge: CUP, 1969) 412–35

Lists bibliographies, collections, the first publication of T's poems to 1897, and criticisms from 1831 to 1967.

107   Campbell, Nancie (comp.)
TENNYSON IN LINCOLN: A CATALOGUE OF THE COLLECTIONS IN THE RESEARCH CENTRE, 2 vols. (Lincoln: The Tennyson Society, vol. I, 1971; vol. II, 1973)

These are the first two of a projected three-volume catalogue of the collections in TRC. Volume I lists books which belonged to the libraries of: T's father, George Clayton Tennyson; T himself; his brother Charles Tennyson-Turner; his son Hallam; and various other members of his family. Volume II lists works by T (including proofs and editions annotated by T) in TRC arranged by date of publication; biography and criticism; and items of Tennysoniana such as pictures, musical settings to his poems, and parodies. It is intended that a third volume will provide an index of the 9,000 letters and other manuscript material in TRC. Unfortunately, many items from TRC had to be sold in 1980; for these, see Sotheby's Sale Catalogue, No. 9341, for Monday and Tuesday, 21 and 22 July 1980. An account of the events of 1979–80 leading to the sale, and of the items which were bought back for retention in TRC as the result of a fund-raising appeal, is given by R. A. Carroll, 'The Tennyson Sales', *TRB* (1980) 141–6. See also Rowland L. Collins, 'Tennyson Manuscripts at the University of Rochester', *TRB* (1984) 134.

108   Allsobrook, Sian (comp.) and Revell, Peter (ed.)
A CATALOGUE OF THE TENNYSON COLLECTION
IN THE LIBRARY OF UNIVERSITY COLLEGE,
CARDIFF (Cardiff: University College, Cardiff, 1972)

This is an efficient record of books purchased from the estate of
Professor Cyril Brett, totalling 416 items and including a very
nearly complete sequence of the pre-1900 editions of T's individual volumes.

109   Madden, Lionel
'Tennyson: A Reader's Guide' and 'Tennyson: A Select
Bibliography', TENNYSON (Writers and Their Background
Series) ed. D. J. Palmer (London: Bell & Sons, 1973) 1–22;
255–65

The first of these items is an excellently readable and judicious
account which discusses most aspects of Tennyson scholarship
and includes comments on texts, biographies, research materials and criticism. Madden summarises the main critical tenden-
cies since Nicolson. The second item complements the first by
listing a brief but helpful selection of works which covers: (1)
Texts; (2) Bibliographies, Dictionaries & Concordance; (3)
Descriptions of Special Collections; (4) Biographical Studies;
(5) General Critical Studies; and (6) Studies of Individual
Works and Groups.

110   Madden, Lionel
'Sir Charles Tennyson: An Annotated Bibliography of His
Published Writings', *TSM* No 6 (Lincoln: The Tennyson
Society, 1973). See also 'A Supplement to the Bibliography
of Sir Charles Tennyson', *TRB* (1977) 6–9

111   McSweeney, Kerry
'The State of Tennyson Criticism', *Papers in Language and
Literature* 10 (1974) 433–46

Updates Johnson (105) by reviewing a particularly rich harvest
of critical works on T in the early 1970s: Ricks (124), Priestley
(211), Palmer (125), Sinfield (293), Reed (366), Eggers (369) *et
al.*

112   Shaw, W. David
       'A Bibliographical Essay', TENNYSON'S STYLE (Ithaca,
       New York: Cornell UP, 1976)

       A slightly idiosyncratic but stimulating and incisive selection
       arranged in two parts: the first 'examines elements of Ten-
       nyson's poetry under five [six] general headings: style and
       thought; poetic development; Victorian poetic theory; knowl-
       edge of rhetoric; generic experiments; and dissociation of
       sensibility . . . The second part is concerned with works of
       scholarship and criticism devoted to individual poems and
       categories of poems'.

113   Beetz, Kirk H.
       TENNYSON: A BIBLIOGRAPHY, 1827–1982 (Scarecrow
       Author Bibliographies No. 68) (Metuchen, New Jersey and
       London: The Scarecrow Press, 1984)

       This has over 5,000 entries, lists the publication of T's major
       volumes and gives an almost complete listing of critical works
       about his writing to 1982. It proceeds chronologically and the
       entries for each year are arranged under Books, Dissertations
       (when relevant) and Periodicals, including reviews and review
       articles. Brief comments are appended to entries the author
       considers significant. It is invaluable as a reference work.

114   ALFRED LORD TENNYSON: A CHRONOLOGY
       (Lincoln: Lincolnshire Recreational Services, County Library
       Department, 1984)

       This useful and attractive pamphlet, which includes photo-
       graphs, drawings and a genealogical table, records the publica-
       tion of T's major works and gives an account of his family,
       friends and publishers.

       Note: Since its inception in 1963, *Victorian Poetry* has included
       each year a 'Guide to the Year's Work in Victorian Poetry'
       which reviews criticism published the previous year. Since
       1974, an entire section of the Guide has been devoted to
       Tennyson.
          Similarly, the *Year's Work in English Studies* has a section on
       Victorian verse which offers a commentary on criticism on
       Tennyson published in the designated year.

Criticism of the Poems

General full-length studies and collections

115   Collins, John Churton
ILLUSTRATIONS OF TENNYSON (London: Chatto and
Windus, 1891)

This book summarises a series of articles by Collins (whom T is
reputed to have called 'a louse upon the locks of scholarship') in
the *Cornhill Magazine* in 1880 and 1881, in which he described
T as a member of the 'class of poets who are essentially imitative
and reflective'. T's copy of the *Cornhill* articles (TRC) is heavily
annotated, mostly to refute Collins's suggestions of parallels
between T's verse and that of previous poets. (For a summary
of T's *Cornhill* annotations, see H. P. Sucksmith, 'Tennyson on
the Nature of his Own Poetic Genius', *Renaissance and Modern
Studies* 11 (1967) 84–9.) Some of Collins's comments are fat-
uous but he was a man of immense literary learning, particularly of the Classics, and his commentary does reveal the
resonant debt T owed to the literature of previous ages. Collins
wrote in the belief that respect for a work was increased by the
kind of comparative criticism he was engaged upon, and also
that it was impossible for recent writers not to echo their
forebears; 'We moderns are "the heirs to all the ages" '. For an
account of Collins's career, see Phyllis Grosskurth, 'Churton
Collins: Scourge of the Late Victorians', *UTQ* 24 (1965)
254–68.

116   Walters, J. Cuming
TENNYSON: POET, PHILOSOPHER, IDEALIST
(London: Kegan Paul, Trench, Trübner, 1893; reprinted New
York: Haskell House, 1971)

Of historical interest as one of the first studies after T's death to
give a serious account of his work as a whole. *In Memoriam* is
highly esteemed – 'no literary work has done more to resolve
doubt . . . and "justify the ways of God to man" ' – whereas
Idylls is regarded as flawed in its conception of Arthur as cold
and colourless.

117   Harrison, Frederic
      'Tennyson', TENNYSON, RUSKIN, MILL (London:
      Macmillan, 1899)

      Of interest as the opinion of a Positivist thinker who considered
      T as a poet who had no philosophical originality but who
      'followed, rather than created, the current ideas of his time'; *In
      Memoriam* is a 'kind of glorified *Christian Year*'.

118   Fausset, Hugh I'Anson
      TENNYSON. A MODERN PORTRAIT (New York:
      Appleton, 1923; reissued New York: Russell and Russell,
      1968)

      A bitter post-war attack on T as a leading representative of the
      Victorian period. 'His morality was a mere projection of his
      senses, seeking to justify before his conscience a state of
      pleasure which he wished to perpetuate. [He had] the selfish
      instincts of the favoured class to which he belonged . . The
      result of such idle high-mindedness was the catastrophe of
      savagery and folly which we have known, and the decimating of
      a generation, young in hope and generosity, which of itself had
      willed no such thing.'

119   Baum, Paull F.
      TENNYSON SIXTY YEARS AFTER (N. Carolina: N.
      Carolina UP, 1948; reprinted London: Archon Books, 1963)

      Described by Baum as 'an interim report on Tennyson's ulti-
      mate position as a poet', this is an interesting example of
      judgemental criticism which sees T as an 'innocent' aesthete
      striving for relevance and thereby beautifying inferior material.
      Baum's criticism is intelligent, rigorous and excellently docu-
      mented but often carping and sometimes contradictory in its
      desire to prove that 'we see [T's] limitations overshadowing his
      accomplishments'. Baum admits to a grudging admiration for
      In Memoriam in spite of 'too much variety, both of style and of
      content'; in its confessional reflectiveness it is a 'remarkably
      frank and disarming revelation . . . a long lyrical domestic
      idyll'.

120   Tennyson, Charles
        SIX TENNYSON ESSAYS (London: Cassell & Co., 1954)

        This contains: (1) 'Tennyson as a Humourist'; (2) 'Tennyson's
        Politics'; (3) 'Tennyson's Religion'; (4) 'Tennyson's Versifica-
        tion'; (5) 'Some MSS of the *Idylls of the King* and a Note on
        Tennyson as a Narrative Poet'; and (6) 'On Reading Tennyson'.

121   Buckley, Jerome Hamilton
        TENNYSON: THE GROWTH OF A POET (Cambridge,
        Mass.: HUP; London: OUP, 1960)

        A benign and balanced coverage of the T canon which places
        the poems in a biographical context: 'T's life was his work; the
        story of his career . . . is the bibliography of his poems'. Useful
        as an introduction to T's poetry, and welcome and pioneering in
        its time as a corrective to the public-versus-private view of T.
        Buckley argues that T was 'the voice and sometimes the cons-
        cience of Victorian culture', but this did not lead him to sacrifice
        personal vision to public esteem; his development depended
        'on the constant interaction between public knowledge and
        private feeling'. This book develops and modifies views ad-
        vanced in 'Tennyson – The Two Voices', *The Victorian Temper:
        A Study in Literary Culture*, 1951, pp. 66–86.

122   Killham, John (ed.)
        CRITICAL ESSAYS ON THE POETRY OF TENNYSON
        (London: Routledge & Kegan Paul, 1960)

        This collection of essays, written since 1936, is still the most
        distinguished and useful collection of critical writings on T, and
        an important factor in rehabilitating T's reputation as a poet
        whom critics should take seriously. Its introduction by John
        Killham gives a 'Review of Modern Criticism' (102). It also
        contains: G. M. Young, 'The Age of Tennyson' (153); Arthur
        J. Carr, 'Tennyson as a Modern Poet', (139); Marshall
        McLuhan, 'Tennyson and Picturesque Poetry' and 'Tennyson
        and the Romantic Epic'; G. Robert Stange, 'Tennyson's
        Garden of Art: A Study of "The Hesperides" ' (232); Elizabeth
        Hillman Waterston, 'Symbolism in Tennyson's Minor Poems';
        Lionel Stevenson, ' "The High-Born Maiden" Symbol in Ten-
        nyson' (230); G. Robert Stange, 'Tennyson's Mythology: A
        Study of "Demeter and Persephone" ' (390); W. W. Robson,
        'The Dilemma of Tennyson' (391); E. J. Chiasson, 'Tennyson's

"Ulysses" – A Reinterpretation' (233); Cleanth Brooks, 'The Motivation of Tennyson's Weeper' (229); Graham Hough, ' "Tears, Idle Tears" ' (231); Leo Spitzer, ' "Tears, Idle Tears" Again'; T. S. Eliot, 'Tennyson's *In Memoriam*' (278); John Killham, 'Tennyson's *Maud* – The Function of the Imagery'; F. E. L. Priestley, 'Tennyson's *Idylls*' (351).

123   Pitt, Valerie
       TENNYSON LAUREATE (London: Barrie and Rockliff, 1962)

Another readable and restorative attempt to correct the 'distorted' view of T as a good private poet and a poor public one. Pitt traces the development in T of a personality which maintains its coherence within changing social requirements, and she asserts his 'reasonableness', credits him with meaning what he says and stresses the variety and originality of his evolving style. But towards the end, even Pitt bows to critical fashion in discerning a dislocation between T and 'a cultural situation unpropitious to literature'.

124   Ricks, Christopher
       TENNYSON (London: Macmillan (Masters of World Literature Series), 1972)

This highly recommended book, a by-product of Ricks's excellent edition of *Poems* (92), is a critical study which selects important experiences in T's private life, particularly in his childhood, and relates them with great insight and sensitivity to recurrent themes and modes of writing in his poetry. Ricks's brilliant attention to the details of the poems gives rise to generalisations which have become critical commonplaces, in particular the notion of T as a master of 'the art of the penultimate'.

125   Palmer, D. J. (ed.)
       TENNYSON (Writers and Their Background Series)
       (London: George Bell & Sons, 1973)

A collection of new essays in a series usefully designed to present major authors 'in their intellectual, social, and artistic contexts'. The volume begins with a chronological table of the main events of T's life in relation to the contemporary scene. Its other contributions are: Lionel Madden, 'Tennyson: A Reader's Guide' (109); D. J. Palmer, 'Tennyson's Romantic Heritage' (174); M. Shaw, 'Tennyson and His Public 1827–1859'; John D. Jump, 'Tennyson's Religious Faith and Doubt'; Philip Drew, 'Tennyson and the Dramatic Monologue: A Study of *Maud*' (334); John Killham, 'Tennyson and Victorian Social Values' (145); John Dixon Hunt, ' "Story Painters and Picture Writers": Tennyson's *Idylls* and Victorian Painting'; Sir Charles Tennyson, 'Tennyson as Poet Laureate'; Peter Thomson, 'Tennyson's Plays and Their Production' (424); Lionel Madden, 'Tennyson: A Select Bibliography' (109).

126   Turner, Paul
        TENNYSON (London, Henley, Boston: Routledge & Kegan Paul, 1976)

A distinguished study, particularly useful on T's classical inheritance and his special gift for adapting previous literature to purposes of self-expression. Turner also writes elegantly and incisively on T's relatedness to his own historical conditions.

127   Culler, A. Dwight
        THE POETRY OF TENNYSON (New Haven and London: Yale UP, 1977)

This provides a chronological survey of T's poetry beginning in leisurely fashion with four chapters on the early poetry and making a somewhat hasty exit with only sixty-odd pages given to the poetry from *Maud* onwards. A rather slackly argued book, it appears to have no overall thesis but to be a series of separate discussions (perhaps a lecture series?) of individual poems or groups of poems.

128   Francis, Elizabeth A. (ed.)
        TENNYSON: A COLLECTION OF CRITICAL ESSAYS (Englewood Cliffs, New Jersey: Prentice-Hall (Twentieth Century Views), 1980)

These essays follow the chronology of T's poems and in most cases are chapters from books, sometimes retitled: W. David Shaw, 'Rites of Passage: "The Lady of Shalott" and "The Lotos-Eaters" ' (from *Tennyson's Style* (214)); Harold Bloom,

'Tennyson: In the Shadow of Keats' (from *Poetry and Repression* (175)); Christopher Ricks, 'Poems from Hallam's Death till the End of 1834' (from *Tennyson* (124)); A. Dwight Culler, 'The English Idyls' (from *The Poetry of Tennyson* (127)); F. E. L. Priestley, 'Style and Genre: *The Princess*' (from *Language and Structure in Tennyson's Poetry* (211)); James Kissane, 'Tennyson: The Passion of the Past and the Curse of Time' (239); T. S. Eliot, 'Tennyson's *In Memoriam*' (278); Alan Sinfield, '*In Memoriam*: The Linnet and the Artefact' (from *The Language of Tennyson's 'In Memoriam'* (293)); Jerome H. Buckley, 'Maud' (from *Tennyson: The Growth of a Poet* (121)); John Rosenberg, '*Idylls of the King*: Evolving Form' (from *The Fall of Camelot* (374)); Elizabeth A. Francis, 'Late Poems', a new essay discussing 'the middle voice of grief' T uses in 'Frater Ave Atque Vale' and in *Demeter and Other Poems* as 'an accommodation with the necessity of endings'.

129   Tennyson, Hallam (ed.)
      STUDIES IN TENNYSON (London and Basingstoke: Macmillan, 1981)

A collection of nine essays based on a series of lectures intended to commemorate the centenary of Sir Charles Tennyson, the poet's grandson, who died aged 97 in 1977; the series of lectures still took place, however. The collection comprises: (i) Hallam Tennyson, 'Charles Tennyson: A Personal Memoir'; (ii) R. B. Martin, 'Charles Tennyson: Writer and Scholar'; (iii) W. W. Robson, 'The Present Value of Tennyson'; (iv) Christopher Ricks, 'Tennyson Inheriting the Earth' (on T's borrowings and self-borrowings); (v) Theodore Redpath, 'Tennyson and the Literature of Greece and Rome'; (vi) Philip Collins, 'Tennyson In and Out of Time'; (vii) Michael Mason, 'The Timing of *In Memoriam*'; (viii) William E. Fredeman, 'One Word More – on Tennyson's Dramatic Monologues'; and (ix) John Bayley, 'Tennyson and the Idea of Decadence' (on the 'polished impersonality' of T's verse).

130   Hair, Donald S.
      DOMESTIC AND HEROIC IN TENNYSON'S POETRY
      (Toronto: University of Toronto Press, 1981)

A thoroughgoing and sometimes laboured account of T as a poet who idealised domestic contentment and made brilliant use of current notions concerning the home and family. Hair begins with a reading of *In Memoriam* as domestic elegy in which loss and grief, and the heroic recovery from grief, are expressed in familial terms. T's poetry up to and beyond *In Memoriam* is then exhaustively examined as a development from a view of domesticity as a social ideal to its symbolic extension as a vision of moral and spiritual harmony.

131   Pinion, F. B.
A TENNYSON COMPANION (London and Basingstoke: Macmillan, 1984)

Difficult to know the readership for whom this book was written: neither popular nor scholarly, it perfunctorily goes over the facts of T's life (relying heavily on Martin) and then gives plot summaries of the poems with critical comments of a dogmatic and often commonplace kind. It contains sixteen pages of illustrations, including photographs and sketches of Farringford and Aldworth.

132   Bloom, Harold (ed.)
ALFRED LORD TENNYSON (Modern Critical Views) (New York: Chelsea House Publishers, 1985)

This is Bloom's 'representative selection of the best criticism devoted to T during the last half-century'. It usefully reprints essays and extracts to give a comprehensive coverage of both T's output and differing critical approaches. It comprises: Harold Bloom, Introduction; T. S. Eliot, 'Tennyson's *In Memoriam*' (278); G. M. Young, 'The Age of Tennyson' (153); Cleanth Brooks, 'The Motivation of Tennyson's Weeper' (229); Marshall McLuhan, 'Tennyson and Picturesque Poetry'; Robert Langbaum, 'The Dynamic Unity of *In Memoriam*' (292); Christopher Ricks, ' "The Days That Are No More" '; John Rosenberg, '*Idylls of the King*: Evolving Form' (374); John Hollander, 'Tennyson's Melody'; Harold Bloom, 'Tennyson: In the Shadow of Keats' (175); A. Dwight Culler, ' "Maud or the Madness" '; Robert Bernard Martin, 'Silent Voices, 1890–1892'.

133   Albright, Daniel
TENNYSON, THE MUSES' TUG-OF-WAR (Charlottesville: UP of Virginia (Virginia Victorian Studies), 1986)

An eclectic, thematically (rather than chronologically) ordered, wayward and colourfully written variant of the 'two-voices' approach to T which diagnoses a 'headache of inaccurate focus' in his poetry deriving from an attempt to unite two incompatible poetics, the transcendental and the materialist. The quest for Romantic sublimity, the imaginative process, the creation and dissolution of personality, the apotheosis of perfected human types – all these issues are ingeniously, if not always convincingly, considered in relation to this divided aesthetic. Albright culminates with chapters on 'The Three Major Poems' – *Maud*, *In Memoriam* and *The Princess* – as 'assaults on the inexpressible', through mythologising in *Maud*, displacement in *In Memoriam* and the fabular in *The Princess*.

134   Thomson, Alastair W.
THE POETRY OF TENNYSON (London and New York: Routledge & Kegan Paul, 1986)

The author says that this is 'not, in any sense, a radical revision of generally accepted opinions about Tennyson', and it is indeed a basic, introductory survey of the poems which describes and evaluates them rather than subjects them to formal criticism or innovative interpretation. Perhaps a useful beginners' book. For a more lively and critically searching introductory study of the poems (although it does not include discussion of *Idylls of the King*) see Roger Ebbatson's modestly priced *Tennyson* (Penguin Critical Studies) (Harmondsworth, Middlesex: Penguin, 1988).

135   Sinfield, Alan
ALFRED TENNYSON (Oxford: Basil Blackwell (Rereading Literature Series, ed. Terry Eagleton), 1986)

A Marxist, deconstructive reading, lively, contentious and iconoclastic, which undertakes to locate T's poetry 'in its ideological field – the range of ideas and attitudes brought into play by the text'. Sinfield investigates the politics of class and gender which inform T's verse, the melancholy which derives from a sense of the inability of language to restore what is lost or to ensure the subjectivity of the speaker, and the verbal strategies by which T strove to bridge the gap between language and reality.

136   Jordan, Elaine
       ALFRED TENNYSON (Cambridge: CUP (British and Irish
       Authors, Introductory Critical Studies), 1988)

       This is a thoughtful and leisurely study, thoroughly researched,
       replete with close readings of the poems yet with a strong
       impulse to place T's poetry in its cultural context. Its appeal lies
       in a personalised approach which is affectionate, deeply knowl-
       edgeable and critically alert. Intended as an introduction for
       students, it will also provide experienced critics with new
       insights and fresh ways of viewing familiar material and ideas.
       Jordan shows a particular concern with gender issues in T's
       poetry and with his testing of the validity and stability of
       language as an expressive and communicative medium. In a
       largely chronological movement through the poems, she dis-
       cusses T's fruitful cultivation of poetic androgyny in the early
       poems, his head-on engagement with the 'woman question' in
       The Princess, the haunting sense of lack which empowers the
       language of *In Memoriam* and the repression and nihilism of
       Idylls of the King.

General articles and chapters

137   Grierson, Herbert J. C.
       'The Tennysons', THE CAMBRIDGE HISTORY OF
       ENGLISH LITERATURE, ed. A. W. Ward and A. R.
       Waller (Cambridge: CUP, 1916), vol. XIII, 23–48

       T's poetry is to that of the great Romantics 'much as a garden to
       a natural landscape' and issues from the conflict between 'his
       sensitive and conservative temperament and that Lucretian
       vision of the universe which physical science seemed more and
       more to unroll'. Grierson doesn't like either *Maud* or *Idylls of
       the King*, the latter being a reflection of 'the worst features of
       the Victorian age'. The comments on the poetry of Frederick
       and Charles are comparatively benign.

138   Leavis, F. R.
       ' "Thought" and Emotional Quality: Notes in the Analysis of
       Poetry', *Scrutiny* XIII (1945–6) 53–71

       This is the famous essay which contrasts 'Tears, Idle Tears' with
       Lawrence's 'Piano', finding T to be self-indulgent, complacent

and unsubtle as a poet, a purveyor of 'emotion for its own sake without a justifying situation'. Similar damaging remarks by this influential critic are to be found in *New Bearings in English Poetry* (1932) (which praises Hopkins at T's expense) and *The Common Pursuit* (1952).

139 Carr, Arthur J.
'Tennyson as a Modern Poet', *UTQ* XIX (1950) 361–82, in Killham (122)

One of the finest essays which suggestively argues for T's modernity as a poet of melancholia and frustration who consistently faced the problem of tragedy in modern art: 'No English poet explored more widely the range of possibilities that had closed'. Carr's sinuous and wide-ranging discussion seems, in a short space, to get to the heart of T's poetry even though, in keeping with the views of his time, Carr sees T as the maimed victim of a cultural crisis. What irradiates Carr's criticism is his sense of T's nobility as a poet 'whose injury cannot be healed and who makes of it, by force of will, the secret of his strength'.

140 Johnson, E. D. H.
'Tennyson', THE ALIEN VISION OF VICTORIAN POETRY. SOURCES OF THE POETIC IMAGINATION IN TENNYSON, BROWNING, AND ARNOLD (Princeton, New Jersey: Princeton UP, 1952) 3–68

Johnson's thesis is that most eminent Victorian writers were 'at odds with their age, and . . . appealed not *to* but *against* the prevailing mores of that age'. An influential exponent of the 'two-voices' school of thought, he sees T as a victim of a 'double awareness' which recognises a 'tragic incompatibility between the life of the imagination and the ways of the world'.

141 House, Humphry
'Tennyson and the Spirit of the Age', ALL IN DUE TIME (London: Rupert Hart-Davies, 1955) 122–9

Less poetically assured than Keats, T was 'haunted by a sense of time' and a consciousness of modernity that led him into didacticism and an identification with externality as a measure of stability.

142   Yeats, W. B.
'The Symbolism of Poetry', ESSAYS AND
INTRODUCTIONS (London: Macmillan, 1961) 153–64

Written in 1900, this essay signalled a modern, and Modernist,
preoccupation with the 'pure' poetry of symbolism and a rejec-
tion of the didactic, ornate and 'cosmic' features which were
thought to disfigure Victorian verse. Yeats calls for 'a casting
out of descriptions of nature for the sake of nature, of the moral
law for the sake of the moral law, a casting out of all anecdotes
and that brooding over scientific opinion that so often ex-
tinguished the central flame in Tennyson'.

143   Ricks, Christopher
'Tennyson's Methods of Composition', *Proceedings of the
British Academy, 1966–7* (London: British Association, 1967)
209–30

The text of Ricks's Chatterton Lecture, this is primarily a plea
for the lifting of the interdict on the Trinity manuscripts but also
contains shrewd critical comments, particularly on T's self-
borrowings which were 'not a convenience but a cast of mind'.

144   Auden, W. H.
'The Poet of No More', *Listener* 88 (August 1972) 181

Reviewing Ricks (124) as 'the best study of Tennyson I have
read', Auden reiterates his earlier view (88) that 'in depicting
states of melancholy or desertion, Tennyson is the greatest poet
who ever lived' and adds: 'To me, his most amazing achievement is that, even in his bleakest poems, there is no trace of self-
pity'.

145   Killham, John
'Tennyson and Victorian Social Values', in Palmer (125) 147–
79

Richly discusses 'Enoch Arden' and other of T's English Idyls,
The Princess and *Maud* in relation to contemporary issues such
as commercialism, the woman question, and patriotism as
debated by Ruskin, Mill and other Victorian sages.

146   Joseph, Gerhard
        'Tennyson's Optics: The Eagle's Gaze', *PMLA* 92 (1977)
        420–8

        'It is the distance that charms me', T said. Although he is often
        regarded as the poet of the 'particularized and the nearby', he
        was also fascinated by the 'exotically distanced in space and the
        remote in time'. Joseph discusses the 'dialectical optics' of T's
        vision between the specific and the vaguely generalised, and
        sees it as a typically Victorian epistemological dilemma.

147   Buckler, William E.
        'A Precarious Turning: Tennyson's Redemption of Literature
        and Life from Medievalism', *BIS* 8 (1980) 85–102

        An invigorating, sometimes hectic, tribute to T. as a major poet
        who 'altered the atmosphere in which poetry subsists'. Buckler
        claims that in his poems T. parleyed between the supreme
        influences of Homer and Dante and finally, in *Idylls*, redeemed
        the poetic imagination from 'the imperious enticements of the
        metaphor of medievalism' to affirm a severely honed classicism
        more suited to the tragic and heroic perceptions of a modern
        age.

148   Mermin, Dorothy
        'Tennyson', THE AUDIENCE IN THE POEM: FIVE
        VICTORIAN POETS (New Brunswick, New Jersey:
        Rutgers UP, 1983)

        Uncertainty concerning the poet's role in the Victorian period,
        and competition from the novel, produced a group of poems
        unusual in English literature in including an auditor, or audi-
        tors, from whom the speaker requires a response: 'not as a
        consequence of the completed utterance but while he is speak-
        ing', and which modifies the speaker's utterance and course of
        action. Mermin claims that 'St. Simeon Stylites' inaugurated
        this mode of discourse, one which T made increasingly sophist-
        icated use of in 'Ulysses', 'Tiresias', 'Tithonus', *Maud* and 'The
        Holy Grail'.

149   Ford, George H.
        ' "A Great Poetical Boa-Constrictor" ', Alfred Tennyson: An
        Educated Victorian Mind', VICTORIAN LITERATURE

AND SOCIETY, ESSAYS PRESENTED TO RICHARD
D. ALTICK (Columbus, Ohio: Ohio State UP, 1984) 146–67

An amiable survey of T's education and learning which seeks to
refute Auden's charge of stupidity by showing T to have
breadth of knowledge and supple-mindedness, and which finds
him to be a creditable example of an educated Victorian.

Context and reputation

150   Chesterton, G. K.
'The Great Victorian Poets', THE VICTORIAN AGE IN
LITERATURE (London: Williams & Norgate [1913]) 160–9

Of many such books around the turn of the century, this seems
to hold its port-wine flavour well. Although Chesterton gave
precedence to the novelists and believed Victorian poetry
defective, he is grandly contemptuous of those who try to
discredit T and has thought-provoking things to say, such as
that T was 'a provincial Virgil' and that although like 'almost
every other Victorian poet, he was really two poets, [in his case]
both the poets were good'.

151   Bradley, A. C.
THE REACTION AGAINST TENNYSON (London:
English Association Pamphlet No. 39, 1917)

'. . . the nadir of [T's] fame may not quite be reached, but it can
hardly be far off. To care for his poetry is to be old-fashioned,
and to belittle it is to be in the movement'. Bradley blames T's
middle-class popularity for the current reaction, and also his
conventional morality. Although generally defensive of T,
Bradley believes *Idylls* is a failure because of its shadowy
characterisation.

152   Bowden, Marjorie
TENNYSON IN FRANCE (Manchester: Manchester UP,
1930)

Where and to what extent T was appreciated in France, the
development of that appreciation, and the part T's poetry

played in forming French poetic outlook towards the end of the century.

153 Young, G. M.
'The Age of Tennyson', *Proceedings of the British Academy*
XXV (1939) 125–42, in Killham (122) and Bloom (132)

A generous and relaxed evocation of T's contemporary appeal, particularly as a poet of nature who, 'in phrases of faultless precision', brought to his increasingly urban and suburban readership 'pictures of the world from which it was exiled and in which it yearned to keep at least an imaginary footing'.

154 Eidson, John Olin
TENNYSON IN AMERICA: HIS REPUTATION AND
INFLUENCE FROM 1827 TO 1858 (Athens, Georgia:
University of Georgia Press, 1943)

A readable account of T's rise to popularity from an exclusive notoriety among the so-called Transcendental School of writers at Harvard, to the publication of *Poems* of 1842 by W. D. Ticknor, the sensational popularity of *The Princess*, the growth of a Tennysonian school of poetry (Lowell, Longfellow, Poe) and the mixed response to *Maud*. Eidson ends with a brief forward look at T's even greater success with *Idylls* and 'Enoch Arden' before the inevitable backlash which occurred in America as well as in England.

155 Green, Joyce
'Tennyson's Development During the "Ten Years'
Silence" ', *PMLA* 66 (1951) 662–97

In meticulous detail, this relates T's 1830 and 1832 volumes to the comments of the reviewers and to the revisions of early poems published in *Poems* (1842). Green moderates Shannon's view (expressed in 'Tennyson and the Reviewers, 1830–1842', *PMLA* 58 (1943) 181–94) that T was profoundly affected by the reviewers. Green believes the evidence suggests that T chastened his style and democratised his themes less from a sycophantic desire to conciliate his critics than from an increasing and independently developed wish to be the chronicler of his age.

156   Shannon, Edgar Finley
        TENNYSON AND THE REVIEWERS: A STUDY OF HIS
        LITERARY REPUTATION AND THE INFLUENCE OF
        THE CRITICS UPON HIS POETRY, 1827–1851
        (Cambridge, Mass.: HUP, 1952)

This influential book argues strongly on the basis of contemporary documentation that T was not so much abused by the
reviewers as had been believed but that they nevertheless had a
profound impact on his abnormally sensitive nature and that he
was influenced by contemporary criticism to a remarkable
extent. Shannon's belief is that T became an instructional poet
under pressure from the reviewers 'to teach more than to
delight'.

157   Davies, Hugh Sykes
        'Lord Tennyson', THE POETS AND THEIR CRITICS, 3
        vols. (London: Hutchinson, 1962), vol. II, BLAKE TO
        BYRON, 243–95

Contains some interesting examples from critics of T from
Hallam to Auden, including Bulwer Lytton's jibes in *The New
Timon* (1846) at 'School-Miss Alfred' and Henry James's account of hearing T read 'Locksley Hall' in 1878: 'I heard [him]
take even more out of his verse than he had put in . . . the point
[was] that he wasn't Tennysonian'. Davies's introduction ex-
emplifies a low point in T's post-war reputation: '[He showed] a
bewilderment as to the true nature of poetry [because] the
serious and workable and worthwhile subject . . . had been
very forcibly taken [from him] by the rise of the novel, the form
of literature which was so naturally and inevitably the product
of the age'.

158   Jump, John D. (ed.)
        TENNYSON: THE CRITICAL HERITAGE (London:
        Routledge & Kegan Paul; New York: Barnes and Noble,
        1967)

An extremely useful collection of thirty-five contemporary
views of T's work from W. J. Fox's review of *Poems, Chiefly
Lyrical* in 1831 to an extract from Collins's *Illustrations of
Tennyson* (1891) (115). Famous criticisms by Hallam (220),
Croker (221), Mill (222), Arnold, Bagehot (203) and Gladstone
(318) are included. There are also extracts from the writings of

Swinburne, Walt Whitman, Taine, Hopkins and R. H. Hutton. The selection illustrates the development of T's reputation and his susceptibility to the opinions of reviewers; it also demonstrates the critical preoccupations of the age.

159   Armstrong, Isabel (ed.)
VICTORIAN SCRUTINIES: REVIEWS OF POETRY
1830–1870 (London: The Athlone Press, 1972)

This examines the preoccupations of Victorian periodical reviewers with the moral function of poetry, its role as an aesthetic rather than a doctrinal teacher and its emphasis on sympathy. Armstrong's selection focuses on 'two occasions when the critical debate was particularly lively and urgent' – the reviews of T's early poetry and of Arnold's 1853 volume and preface. Armstrong reprints reviews of T by W. J. Fox, Hallam, John Wilson, and also C. P. Chretien on *The Princess* and F. Lushington on *In Memoriam*.

160   Collins, Joseph J.
'Tennyson and the Spasmodics', *VN* 43 (Spring 1973) 24–8

Collins argues (against J. H. Buckley in *The Victorian Temper* (1951)) that T was not influenced in the writing of *Maud* by so-called Spasmodic poems such as Alexander Smith's *A Life Drama* (1852) and Sydney Dobell's *Balder* (1853), but rather the other way round; their authors were imitating Spasmodic elements always present in T's work.

161   Joseph, Gerhard
'Poe and Tennyson', *PMLA* 88 (1973) 418–28

Poe described T as 'the *greatest* poet that ever lived' and T admired Poe. Joseph considers the aesthetic principles they had in common which he describes as a 'quest for infinitude'.

162   Scott, P. G.
'John Addington Symonds and the Reaction Against Tennyson', *TRB* (1974) 85–95

Suggests that Symonds' reaction to T, often taken as an instance of the growing hostility towards his poetry from the late 1860s onwards, was more complex and ambivalent than has been believed. See also Robert L. Peters, 'John Addington Symonds: Three Letters to the Tennysons', *TRB* (1981) 192–5.

163   Marshall, George O.
'Tennyson in Parody and Jest: An Essay and a Selection', *TSM* No. 7 (Lincoln: The Tennyson Society, 1975)

As Marshall says, T has been the most parodied of poets and this pamphlet offers examples by W. E. Aytoun and T. Martin, C. S. Calverley, Swinburne and, of course, Anonymous, but not the delectable Lewis Carroll.

164   Tillotson, Kathleen
'Tennyson and Browning: The "Conjunction of Names" ', *TRB* (1976) 177–83

Comments on Browning's slow progress towards acceptance by the reading public alongside T's great popularity during the years from 1855 until 1868 and the enthusiastic reception of *The Ring and the Book*.

165   Mazzeno, Lawrence W.
'Tennyson and Henry James', *TRB* (1979) 111–16

Re-examines and qualifies the evidence around the claim that James was one of the leaders of the reaction against T.

166   Gribble, Jennifer
THE LADY OF SHALOTT IN THE VICTORIAN NOVEL (London: Macmillan, 1983)

Argues that T's poem articulated a myth which provided Victorian novelists with a structure and metaphors for their fiction, particularly in their concern with 'the individual consciousness, its relationship with society, and the nature and role of creative imagination'.

167   Shaw, W. David
THE LUCID VEIL: POETIC TRUTH IN THE VICTORIAN AGE (London: The Athlone Press, 1987)

T features throughout this learned and complex study of the connection between 'Victorian poetics and changing theories of language'. The 'lucid veil', T's phrase from *In Memoriam* 67.14, is used by Shaw to describe the idea of language as a 'screen of analogy' similar to T's conception of the material world, 'where the ladders and symbols are, [as] surely more of a veil which hides the Infinite than a mirror which reveals it'. Shaw ranges among philosophers and epistemologists from Kant to Bradley and discusses the ideas of T and many other Victorian poets and critics in relation to changing theories of language, from the atomism of *laissez-faire* liberalism to the 'darkening glass' of the agnostics.

168   Richards, Bernard
ENGLISH POETRY OF THE VICTORIAN PERIOD
1830–1890 (London and New York: Longman Group
(Longman Literature in English Series, ed. David Carroll
and Michael Wheeler), 1988)

The author points out that 'there has not been a general history of Victorian Poetry since J. Drinkwater's of 1923 and B. I. Evan's of 1933'. This book aims to fill that gap with chapters on 'The Image of the Poet and the Function of Poetry', 'The Diction of Victorian Poetry', 'Victorian Versification', 'Genres', 'The Past', 'Love Poetry', 'Domesticity', 'The Elegiac', 'Victorian Satire', 'Nature and Science', 'Art and Artists', 'Religion', 'The City' and 'Adumbrations of Modernism'. There are also a useful chronology, general bibliographies, and notes on individual authors. It provides an accessible and sensible survey (although with an irritating assumption that poets and readers are invariably male) in which T features throughout.

The Romantic inheritance

169   Bush, Douglas
'Tennyson', MYTHOLOGY AND THE ROMANTIC
TRADITION IN ENGLISH POETRY (Cambridge, Mass.:
HUP, 1937) 197–228

Of the Nicolson era, Bush rejects the Victorian and values only the 'classic' T: '. . . in antique garb Tennyson becomes another man . . . classic themes generally banished from his mind what was timid, parochial, sentimental, inadequately philosophical, and evoked his special gifts and his most authentic emotions, his rich and wistful sense of the past, his love of nature, and his power of style'.

170   Ford, George H.
KEATS AND THE VICTORIANS: A STUDY OF HIS INFLUENCE AND RISE TO FAME, 1821–1895 (New Haven: Yale UP; London: Archon Books, 1944) 17–48

In 'Keats's Debt to Tennyson' Ford discusses the part played by the Apostles in popularising Keats; in 'Tennyson's Debt to Keats' he points out that not only are there definite echoes of Keats in T's poetry but that both poets inhabit the same world of beauty and passion, although T later cultivated 'soundness' and relevance.

171   Ball, Patricia M.
'Tennyson and the Romantics', *VP* 1 (1963) 7–16

Briefly but tellingly argues that T's poetry is best understood in the light of his Romantic inheritance as the development of two egotistical modes in *In Memoriam* and *Maud*: the self that is mediated through love of another and the self that transcends its isolation through accommodation to the demands of others.

172   Ball, Patricia M
'Inheriting Pagasus: Tennyson, Arnold and Browning', THE CENTRAL SELF: A STUDY IN ROMANTIC AND VICTORIAN IMAGINATION (London: Athlone Press, 1968) 166–200

In this interesting study of Victorian developments of the Romantic vision, Ball comments on T's 'chameleon spirit' as similar to the multiple perspectives of the Romantics, but his is a 'colder interpretation of such shifting variety' which gives a sense of a 'menacing split within a single mind'. *In Memoriam* in particular demonstrates 'a crisis of faith in personal identity'.

173   Bloom, Harold
'Tennyson, Hallam and Romantic Tradition', THE

RINGERS IN THE TOWER: STUDIES IN ROMANTIC
TRADITION (Chicago and London: University of Chicago
Press, 1971) 145–54

Hallam was T's Romantic conscience and after his influence
waned 'discursiveness became a Tennysonian vice'. Bloom
speculates on 'how the sensibility of a major Romantic poet was
subverted': his essay includes an insightful discussion of
'Mariana'.

174   Palmer, D. J.
'Tennyson's Romantic Heritage', in Palmer (125) 23–51

A lucid discussion of T's development through the early poems
to *In Memoriam* as 'a Romantic progression from introverted
and inert states of mind to emancipated consciousness'.

175   Bloom, Harold
'Tennyson: In the Shadow of Keats', POETRY AND
REPRESSION (New Haven and London: Yale UP, 1976)
143–74, in Bloom (132) and Francis (128)

A highly individual and intriguing post-structuralist reading of
'Mariana', 'The Hesperides', 'Tithonus', 'Tears, Idle Tears'
and part of 'The Holy Grail' as poems of belatedness and
repression in relation to Keatsian sublimity.

176   McSweeney, Kerry
TENNYSON AND SWINBURNE AS ROMANTIC
NATURALISTS (Toronto, Buffalo, London: University of
Toronto Press, 1981)

McSweeney discusses these two poets' views of, and influence
on, each other and then considers them as types of the Romantic naturalist to whom 'man [is] most creatively alive . . . when
in vital reciprocal contact with the world around him, and . . .
most isolated and anguished when the bond between self and
nature, inner and outer, is broken'. Ten of T's early poems are
analysed to show his negotiation of a post-Romantic mode of
thinking, leading to an acceptance of the cyclical nature of
existence in *In Memoriam* and the vitalist principle which

Arthur embodies in *Idylls of the King*. McSweeney then turns to
a similar examination of Swinburne's poetry.

177   Tucker, Herbert F.
      TENNYSON AND THE DOOM OF ROMANTICISM
      (Cambridge, Mass. and London: HUP, 1988)

An overlong and wordy development of ideas advanced
elsewhere (217, 258, 267) with the addition of new material to
cover the whole range of T's poetry, this aims to provide
exegesis of the poems in Part I and a contextual study in Part II;
in the author's words, it is 'a study that is both historical and
critical'. Its theme is T's dislocated and burdensome relationship to his Romantic predecessors of whom only Coleridge
could provide T with spiritual or poetic guidance.

Religion, philosophy and science

178   Masterman, Charles F. G.
      TENNYSON AS A RELIGIOUS TEACHER (London:
      Methuen, 1900)

An intelligent and well-informed early contribution to the
debate on T as a religious poet. In Masterman's view, all T's
religious speculation rested on the affirmation of 'the reality of
the self' and on a belief in immortality as essential to the upward
development of the human race.

179   Lockyer, Joseph Norman and Lockyer, Winifred L.
      TENNYSON AS A STUDENT AND POET OF NATURE
      (London: Macmillan, 1910)

Still a very useful reference work for anyone interested in the
scientific element in T's writing. The authors comment on T's
'unceasing interest in the causes of things' and on his meticulous
attitude to details of nature.

180   Fairchild, H. N.
      'Tennyson', RELIGIOUS TRENDS IN ENGLISH
      POETRY, VOL. IV: 1830–1880, CHRISTIANITY AND

ROMANTICISM IN THE VICTORIAN ERA (New York:
Columbia UP, 1957) 102–31

Lively, learned and contentious, Fairchild is good on T in
relation to his contemporaries. She concludes that T was 'not a
mystic but an emotional pragmatist'.

181   Stevenson, Lionel
        'Alfred Tennyson', DARWIN AMONG THE POETS (New
        York: Russell and Russell, 1963) 55–116

        'Throughout the period of fiercest controversy between "sci-
        ence" and "religion" Tennyson retained and elaborated his
        compromise between the two which he had constructed before
        the general engagement began'.

182   Forsyth, R. A.
        'The Myth of Nature and the Victorian Compromise of the
        Imagination', *ELH* 31 (1964) 213–40

        Starting from F. W. Bateson's claim that the 'Victorians spoke
        two languages, reflecting the divided aims and origins of their
        civilization: a language of the heart and a language of the head'
        (*English Poetry and the English Language* (1934) p. vi), For-
        syth demonstrates T's 'incipient hostility to Science . . result-
        ing from his dread of its exclusive veracity. This led him to
        compromise the imagination through associating too closely the
        suffering man and the creative poet within himself'.

183   Brashear, William R.
        THE LIVING WILL: A STUDY OF TENNYSON AND
        NINETEENTH CENTURY SUBJECTIVISM (The Hague
        and Paris: Mouton, 1969)

        An interesting discussion of T's poems, particularly *In Memo-
        riam*, *Idylls of the Kings* and 'Lucretius', in relation to the
        thought of Kant, Fichte, Schopenhauer and Nietzsche. Al-
        though no evidence exists that T made a study of these philoso-
        phers, Brashear argues for their common participation in
        nineteenth-century subjectivist attempts to impose the 'living
        will' of Apollonian consciousness upon the Dionysian flux of
        material experience.

184   Millhauser, M.
'Fire and Ice: The Influence of Science on Tennyson's
Poetry', *TSM* No. 4 (Lincoln: The Tennyson Society, 1971)

A well-informed and thoughtful pamphlet pointing out the
recurring importance of scientific images to T and his brooding
preoccupation, which does not basically alter throughout his
career, with the pitiless evidence science offered him concerning the littleness and animality of human beings and the frailty
of faith to withstand these doubts.

185   Rosenberg, John D.
'Tennyson and the Landscape of Consciousness', *VP* 12
(1974) 97–124

All that T ever wrote was informed by a 'double awareness –
matter as rock-solid and matter as mere shadow', and this led to
a double vision of 'hyperclarity [and] a complementary sense of
the external world as alien [and] transient as mist'.

186   Elliott, Philip
'Tennyson and Spiritualism', *TRB* (1979) 89–100

This discusses T's fascinated but finally unconvinced attitude to
spiritualism and its possible influence on his poems.

187   Cosslett, Tess
'Tennyson', 'THE SCIENTIFIC MOVEMENT' AND
VICTORIAN LITERATURE (Brighton: Harvester; New
York: St Martin's Press, 1982)

Examines T's poetry as an example of the Victorian non-
Promethean image of science. Like Tyndall, Huxley and other
members of the Metaphysical Society, T believed in a 'cooper-
ancy' between a scientific and a spiritual explanation of the
world. *In Memoriam* is less anti-scientific than has been believed; it demonstrates an agnostic acceptance of nature's
impermanence while retaining belief in the mystery of ultimate
causation.

188   Shannon, Edgar F.
' "The Thews of Anakim" ': Postulations of the Superhuman
in Tennyson's Poetry', *VQR* 59 (1983) 587–608

Poems from 'Timbuctoo' to 'The Dawn' and 'The Making of

Man' (1892) perused for T's faith in human perfectibility deriving from 'his own inner intimations of the divine element in human beings'.

189   Butts, Richard
        'Languages of Description and Analogy in Victorian Science
        and Poetry', *English Studies in Canada* XI (1985) 193–213

Ranges learnedly from 'The Two Voices' to 'The Ancient Sage' in considering T's contribution to the epistemological debate among Victorian scientists and philosophers concerning modes of understanding, whether univocal or equivocal. Like Tyndall, T recognised a 'Power' behind nature which renders scientific explanation analogous rather than objective in its apprehension of truth.

190   Dean, Dennis R.
        'Tennyson and Geology', *TSM* No. 10 (Lincoln: The
        Tennyson Society, 1985)

Dean very usefully traces the development of geology as a science throughout the nineteenth century, and its popular impact, in relation to T's interest in the subject and use of it in his poetry.

191   Hair, Donald
        'Tennyson's Faith: A Re-examination', *UTQ* 55 (1985/6)
        185–203

Discusses the influence on T of the philosophical traditions represented by Locke and Coleridge and the balance they helped him create between outer evidence and inner need. Locke's insistence that 'knowledge of which we can be certain is limited and insufficient and . . . must be completed by assumptions about . . . a moral order in the universe' is complemented by Coleridge's belief that human needs and wishes should be accorded authority as 'an affirmation of faith because they are a reflection of divine love'.

192   Nichols, Ashton
        'The Epiphanic Trance Poem: Why Tennyson Is Not a
        Mystic', *VP* 24 (1986) 131–48

Claims that T cannot be described as a mystic but that he did have experiences similar to Wordsworth's 'spots of time' and

Browning's 'infinite moment'. These were like modern literary 'epiphanies' in being revelatory experiences firmly grounded in this world, in the mind of the poet, and not from some external power.

Other thematic studies

193   Joseph, Gerhard
       TENNYSONIAN LOVE: THE STRANGE DIAGONAL
       (Minneapolis: University of Minnesota Press, 1969)

The 'strange diagonal' (a phrase from *The Princess*) is T's attempt to synthesise the intellectual cross-currents of his age in which the inheritance of a Platonic dualistic philosophy concerning love was being challenged by the erotic idealism of the Romantics and of Arthur Hallam. Joseph interestingly surveys all the major poems as products of T's own temperament and experience and in their Victorian context of a contradictory 'social assumption [that] the romantic, erotic union of man and woman should take place within the confines of a sacramental and contractual marriage'.

194   Millett, Kate
       Chapter 3, 'The Sexual Revolution, First Phase', SEXUAL
       POLITICS (New York: Doubleday, 1970; London: Rupert
       Hart-Davis, 1971)

Pioneer feminist literary criticism which wittily sets T in the context of nineteenth-century women's movements and the patriarchal attempts, including those by T in *The Princess* and *Idylls*, to contain them.

195   Johnson, Wendell Stacy
       'Marriage and Divorce in Tennyson', SEX AND
       MARRIAGE IN VICTORIAN POETRY (Ithaca and
       London: Cornell UP, 1975) 110–84

Johnson charts a deteriorating view of women from idealisation in the early poems to their symbolic representation in the poems from *Maud* onwards of all that is most dangerous and alien in human nature.

196   Ball, Patricia M.
THE HEART'S EVENTS: THE VICTORIAN POETRY
OF RELATIONSHIPS (London: The Athlone Press, 1976)

A readable and sensitive account of mid-century poetry of
personal relationships which includes discussion of *In Memoriam* and *Maud*. Although the Victorian poets shared an imaginative vision of love with their Romantic predecessors, they
explored 'the implications of loving and being loved with a
thoroughness, a social and personal realism and a sensitivity
which is not found earlier'. *In Memoriam* as a poem of mourning is fruitfully compared with Coventry Patmore's *Odes of
Bereavement*, and *Maud* as a poem of the frustration and
extremism of love with Meredith's *Modern Love* and
Browning's *James Lee's Wife*.

197   Christ, Carol
'Victorian Masculinity and the Angel in the House', A
WIDENING SPHERE, ed. Martha Vicinus (Bloomington,
Indiana: Indian UP, 1977) 146–62

Discusses the difficulty both T and Coventry Patmore experienced in constructing a convincing male ideal in their poetry.
Their unease with the conventional masculine attributes of
aggression and achievement finds an over-compensating complementarity in an idealisation of feminine passivity.

198   Kozicki, Henry
TENNYSON AND CLIO: HISTORY IN THE MAJOR
POEMS (Baltimore and London: John Hopkins UP, 1979)

T's abiding 'Passion of the Past' affiliates him to Clio, the muse
of the meaning and purpose of history, and his philosophy of
history is the unifying intellectual force in his poetry. This
presupposition is the basis of Kozicki's specialised and rather
difficult chronological sweep of the poems which are perceived
as a 'socio-psychological "structure" that underwent growth,
development and decay'. The major poems are examined in
relation to T's preoccupation with divinity, process, and the
individual and collective imperatives, and the progression
through them is seen as generally pessimistic until the late phase
of 'The Higher Pantheism', 'The Voice and the Peak' and
'Vastness', when T's interest in metaphysics helped him to
disengage from the 'historical slough'.

199   Colley, Ann C.
TENNYSON AND MADNESS (Athens, Georgia: Georgia
UP, 1983)

An approachable account of T's acquaintance with mental
instability in the context of nineteenth-century conceptions and
treatment of insanity, and the use he made of this in his poetry
to explore heightened states of consciousness and as a metaphor for social and individual disorder. Colley includes interesting biographical information concerning the management of
T's own neurotic conditions; she then discusses *The Lover's
Tale* and *Maud* as examples of T's portrayal of a form of insanity
the nineteenth century was much concerned with – obsession or
the *idée fixe* – and his more sophisticated metaphysical use of
madness in *Idylls of the King*. Colley's conclusion is that the
threat of madness in T's life was inspirational, requiring control
over excess while subverting routine and the mundane.

200   Basham, Diana
'Tennyson and His Fathers: The Legacy of Manhood in
Tennyson's Poems', *TRB* (1985) 163–78

T wrote no elegy for his father; yet his troubled relationship
with him, and through him with the notions of fatherhood and
manhood, profoundly affected his poetry.

201   Christ, Carol T.
'The Feminine Subject in Victorian Poetry', *ELH* 54
(Summer 1987) 385–401

This discusses a range of T's poems from the point of view of the
'relationship between gender and authorship'. The feminisa-
tion of the poet during the Victorian period created a conflict
concerning the prerogative and power of the gaze; the gratifica-
tions of looking came into conflict with an accompanying sense
of the powerlessness (a symbolic castration) of being looked at.

202   Shaw, Marion
ALFRED LORD TENNYSON (London: Harvester
(Feminist Readings Series), 1988)

This is an attempt to understand the maleness of T's writing and the sexual politics of his poems, in particular how his deteriorating view of heterosexual love derives from psychological determinants at odds with the gender constructs of his time.

Style

203 Bagehot, Walter
'Wordsworth, Tennyson, and Browning; or Pure, Ornate, and Grotesque Art in English Poetry', vol. II of LITERARY STUDIES, 3 vols., ed. Richard Holt, vol. (London: Longmans Green & Co., 1879), extract in Jump (158)

First published in the *National Review* (November 1864) this was a review article of *Enoch Arden, etc.* and Browning's *Dramatis Personae*. It is not only critically provocative but also provides a fascinating insight into Victorian critical preoccupations and methods and illustrates the rise in reputation of Wordsworth's poetry after his death. Bagehot compares the pure style of Wordsworth, which is characterised by 'the least clothing it will admit', with T's ornate style, which has 'the richest and most involved clothing that it will admit': 'nothing is described as it is; everything has about it an atmosphere of something else'. Bagehot blames the lowliness of T's subject matter – 'People who sell fish about the country . . . never are beautiful' – which requires the poet to supplement his paucity of theme with 'a splendid accumulation of impossible accessories'.

204 Mustard, Wilfred P.
CLASSICAL ECHOES IN TENNYSON (New York: Macmillan, 1904)

Mustard records not only the conscious adaptations and borrowings but also points to passages 'where a subtle or unconscious memory of some ancient poet seems to have determined the choice of a word or the turn of a phrase'.

205 Pyre, J. F. A.
THE FORMATION OF TENNYSON'S STYLE: A STUDY, PRIMARILY, OF THE VERSIFICATION OF

THE EARLY POEMS (Madison: Wisconsin UP, 1921; reprinted, 1968)

A detailed, technical analysis of T's style to *In Memoriam*. Pyre's contention is that during the 'ten years' silence' T subdued the irregularity and experimentation of his early verse and 'conventionalized his poetic diction [and] normalized his metres'. Pyre also shows T to be 'a derived poet' whose sources can be identified.

206   Paden, W. D.
TENNYSON IN EGYPT: A STUDY OF THE IMAGERY IN HIS EARLIER WORKS (Lawrence, Kansas: University of Kansas Press, 1942; reprinted 1971)

Using what information was then available, before the establishment of the collection in TRC, Paden's concern was with the sources of T's poetry in his reading in the library at Somersby, particularly as they appear in his contributions to *Poems by Two Brothers* (1827). Although an exercise in source-hunting, Paden's pioneer book was 'essentially an attempt to consider the personality of Tennyson in his youth', especially his often repressed and sublimated erotic preoccupations which were manifest in the works he read and pillaged. These included Sir William Jones's *Moâllakât*, Claude-Etienne Savary's *Letters on Egypt*, Jacob Bryant's *Ancient Mythology* and George Stanley Faber's *The Origin of Pagan Idolatry*. Paden indicates how the exotic imagery T drew from these sources persisted throughout his poetry.

207   Langbaum, Robert
THE POETRY OF EXPERIENCE: THE DRAMATIC MONOLOGUE IN THE MODERN LITERARY TRADITION (London: Chatto and Windus; New York: Norton Library, 1957) 87–93

In this brilliant and influential study of what Langbaum calls 'poetry of sympathy' by which the self is explored through entry into the imagined experience of others, T is discussed briefly but insightfully as a monologuist who 'does not look for extraordinary motives' (as Browning does) but presents emotion with an unnatural intensity morbidly in excess of rational motives. Langbaum discusses 'Ulysses' and other early poems as possessing 'a feeling for the pathology of the emotions'.

208   Fulweiler, Howard W.
'Tennyson and the "Summons from the Sea" ', *VP* 3 (1965)
25–44

An analysis of T's 'shifting use of sea symbolism' throughout his
career from an early use of the sea as 'an introspective and
subjective realm of escape' to its representation as 'a gateway to
religious experience' in poems such as *In Memoriam* and 'The
Holy Grail'.

209   Shaw, W. David and Gartlein, Carl W.
'The Aurora: A Spiritual Metaphor in Tennyson', *VP* 3
(1965) 213–22

T's scientifically correct use of imagery of aurora borealis in
many poems preserved a complex allegiance to both fact and
value, doubt and faith.

210   Dodsworth, Martin
'Patterns of Morbidity: Repetition in Tennyson's Poetry',
THE MAJOR VICTORIAN POETS: A
RECONSIDERATION, ed. Isobel Armstrong (London:
Routledge & Kegan Paul, 1969) 7–34

Persuasively argues (with particularly interesting reference to
Enoch Arden) that T's Wordsworth-like use of repetition is 'the
mark of an inability to progress from one state of feeling to
another, and arises from a sense of inadequacy to express the
strength of feeling experienced'. The reader is drawn into T's
depiction of states of mind that are self-enclosed and
inconclusive.

211   Priestley, F. E. L.
LANGUAGE AND STRUCTURE IN TENNYSON'S
POETRY (London: André Deutsch, 1973)

A lucid and perceptive exploration of T's verbal art through the
major phases of his development from a youthful preoccupation with metre and stanza form to the mature and innovative
experimentations in genre. Priestley includes particularly interesting discussions of *Maud* and *Aylmer's Field*; and in ' "Mean-
ings ambushed": The oblique use of language', he makes a
subtle analysis of 'On a Mourner' in which he suggests that a

surface appearance of directness is at odds with an obliquity of expression, the effect being one of calm suspense.

212 Kincaid, James R.
TENNYSON'S MAJOR POEMS. THE COMIC AND IRONIC PATTERNS (New Haven and London: Yale UP, 1975)

Descries and describes a 'semi-circular pattern' from 'the rich ironic statement' of the early poems to 1842, through the comic strategies of *The Princess*, *In Memoriam* and *Maud*, and back to irony in the darkly unresolved *Idylls of the King*. Kincaid applies Northrop Frye's definition of 'general' or 'open' irony as a narrative pattern which depicts 'dominant opposites which cannot be coordinated or made to cancel, but which demand equal and contradictory responses'. On the other hand, comedy 'transforms an inhibiting condition . . . to a clarified and liberating one'. Within this framework, Kincaid's discussion of the early poems and *In Memoriam* is particularly thoughtful and provocative.

213 Christ, Carol T.
THE FINER OPTIC: THE AESTHETIC OF PARTICULARITY IN VICTORIAN POETRY (New Haven: Yale UP, 1975)

A thoughtful and stimulating study, in which T is discussed throughout, of the preoccupation with the visual in Victorian poetry and the attempt to transcend it. Christ's argument is organised around three 'problems': morbidity, the grotesque, and the good moment. Her discussion is particularly illuminating on T's trance states 'in which the boundaries that delimit the identity of things melt away' and yet the details of those things are seen with obsessional and microscopic exactitude.

214 Shaw, W. David
TENNYSON'S STYLE (Ithaca and London: Cornell UP, 1976)

This excellent book springs from a desire to refute T. S. Eliot's condemnation of T's blank verse as deficient in subtlety and surprise. Shaw substantiates the claim for T that 'no other poet of the nineteenth century commands such a wide range of styles and themes' by a rigorous yet eminently readable analysis of the poems. The basis of his argument is that T combines 'the symbolic form characteristic of Romantic poems with grammatical and rhetorical structures of the kind treated in neoclassic theories'. Shaw's study is informed by extensive knowledge of stylistics and of the Victorian intellectual context, and by a passionate yet judicious admiration for T's poetry.

215   Sinfield, Alan
'Tennyson's Imagery', *Neophilologus* 60 (1976) 466–79

An important and persuasively argued essay which claims that the most subtle feature of T's imagery is the movement between literal and figurative modes of language. Sinfield's sophisticated analysis of erotic imagery in 'Oenone', 'Fatima', 'Lucretius' and *Maud* demonstrate how the two techniques of displacement and fantasy in T's poetry blur the borders between the literal and the figurative.

216   Pattison, Robert
TENNYSON AND TRADITION (Cambridge, Mass. and London: HUP, 1979)

A short, well-written, valuable study of 'the forms Tennyson used . . . why he chose to work with them, and . . . how he evolved these forms in a manner that accorded with his poetic vision'. Pattison's concern is particularly with the creative use T made of the idyll, a form which allowed him to cultivate a 'high degree of objectivity and distance'. The idyll 'moves with, but at a distance from, the drama it describes', and the adoption and manipulation of this form in various guises from the *English Idyls*, through *The Princess*, *In Memoriam* and *Maud* to *Idylls of the King* gave T a control of and perspective on the complex, controversial and suggestive material he chose to write about throughout his career.

217   Tucker, Herbert F.
'Tennyson and the Measure of Doom', *PMLA* 98 (1983) 8–20

T often composed poems 'backwards' (as he said of *Maud*) from a foreordained conclusion; his is the 'poetry of aftermath', a coming to terms with the inevitable. Tucker argues skilfully that the rhetorical tension of T's 'measured language' derives from the struggle for self-definition against the dissolving sense of doom inherent in the terminal situations which are the driving force of his poems.

218   Hughes, Linda K.
THE MANYFACÉD GLASS: TENNYSON'S DRAMATIC MONOLOGUES (Athens, Ohio: Ohio UP, 1987)

T's monologues are concerned with the consciousness of his characters, whereas Browning renders the personality of his. The interiority of the Tennysonian monologue undergoes a 'trajectory of development' which Hughes traces from the early poems to *Idylls of the King* as a movement from intense subjectivity to a public and oracular presence. This familiar thesis is partially revitalised by Hughes's discovery of the use of the monologic form, variously adapted, in most of T's poems.

219   Burnett, Archie
'Echoes and Parallels in Tennyson's Poetry', *NQ* 34 (March 1987) 40–1

Supplements Ricks's annotations (92) of allusions in T's, poetry. Most of Burnett's list are from Shakespeare and Milton.

Criticism of the Early Poetry (1827–47) Including *The Princess*

The volumes of published poems covered by this section are as follows:

Poems by Two Brothers 1827
    (Written with his brother Charles, and a few contributions by his brother Frederick.)
Poems, Chiefly Lyrical 1830
Poems 1832 ('1833')
Poems, 2 vols. 1842
    (Vol. I comprised a selection of poems, considerably revised, from *Poems, Chiefly Lyrical* and *Poems* (1832); vol. II consisted of new poems.)
The Princess 1847
    (In the third edition (1850), Tennyson intercalated six rhymed songs between the sections of the poem. In the fourth edition (1851), Tennyson added passages relating to the prince's 'weird seizures'. The poem reached its final form with the enlargement of the Prologue in the fifth edition in 1853.)

220   [Hallam, A. H.]
      'On Some of the Characteristics of Modern Poetry, and on the Lyrical Poems of Alfred Tennyson, *Poems, Chiefly Lyrical*', *Englishman's Magazine* I (August 1831) 616–28, in Jump (158) and Hunt (290)

The famous review which maintains that there are two kinds of poets, the poet of reflection, characterised by Wordsworth, and the poet of sensation of whom Keats and Shelley are examples. Hallam places T in the latter category and lavishes praise on the 'five distinctive excellences' of his poetry: luxuriance of imagination; 'his power of embodying himself in ideal characters'; a 'vivid, picturesque delineation of objects'; metrical variety; and elevation of thought. The review provoked the wrath of the Tory reviewers, particularly J. W. Croker whose sarcastic riposte in the *Quarterly* (221) may have contributed to T's 'silence' between 1832 and 1842. Subsequently the review has

generally been seen as representing T's 'Romantic conscience'.
See Eileen Tess Johnston, 'Hallam's Review of Tennyson: its
Contexts and Significance', *TSLL* 23 (1981) 1–26.

221   [Croker, John Wilson]
[Review of] '*Poems* [1832]', *Quarterly Review* 49 (April 1833)
81–96, in Jump (158)

A deeply scornful and vituperative review which allegedly
affected T profoundly (*Memoir* I 94–7) and contributed to 'the
ten years' silence'.

222   [Mill, John Stuart]
[Review of] '*Poems, Chiefly Lyrical* and *Poems*', *London
Review* I (July 1835) 402–24, in Jump (158)

T found this review 'a great encouragement' (*Memoir* I 122); it
continued Hallam's notion of T as a poet of sensation but also
stressed the need for 'continual study and meditation' to give a
philosophical depth to his poetry.

223   [Sterling, John]
'On Tennyson's Poems', *Quarterly Review* LXX (September
1842) 385–416, in Jump (158)

Supposedly responsible for T's tardiness in writing more
Arthurian poetry, this review commented of 'Morte d'Arthur'
that 'the miraculous legend of Excalibur does not come very
near to us, and, as reproduced by any modern writer, must be a
mere ingenious exercise of fancy'.

224   [Masson, David]
[Review of] '*Poems* (4th edn 1848) and *The Princess*', *North
British Review* XVII (1848) 43–72.

This review-article on the role and nature of contemporary
poetry interprets *The Princess* as an allegory in which Ida
represents Intellect erroneously striving to exist in isolation.
Masson, who was one of the most respected critics of the time,
complains that there is no 'distinct connexion between the

greater portion of [the poem's] details, and [this] central thought'.

225   [Marston, J. W.]
       [Review of] '*The Princess*', *Athenaeum* XXI (January 1848)
       6–8, in Jump (158)

This review by Marston, who was a dramatist, set the note of much subsequent reviewing of *The Princess*: 'The grand error of the story is the incoherency of its characteristics. Its different parts refuse to amalgamate.'

226   Dawson, S. E.
       A STUDY, WITH CRITICAL AND EXPLANATORY
       NOTES, OF ALFRED TENNYSON'S POEM *THE
       PRINCESS* (Montreal: Dawson Bros., 1882; second edn,
       1884, includes a letter from T to Dawson)

T's letter is reproduced in Eversley and is primarily concerned to correct the impression Dawson gives that T's allusions to earlier writers were precise and particular. Otherwise, T agrees with Dawson's comments, especially his opinion that 'if women ever were to play such freaks, the burlesque and the tragic might go hand in hand'.

227   Pyre, J. F. A.
       THE FORMATION OF TENNYSON'S STYLE: A
       STUDY, PRIMARILY, OF THE VERSIFICATION OF
       THE EARLY POEMS (Madison: Wisconsin UP, 1921;
       reprinted 1968)

See (205).

228   Howell, A. C.
       'Tennyson's "Palace of Art"': An Interpretation', *Studies in
       Philology* 33 (1936) 507–22

Howell's ingenious and engaging argument is that the Palace of Art is Cambridge and that the poem represents T's disenchant-ment with its élitism and stagnation.

229   Brooks, Cleanth
        'The Motivation of Tennyson's Weeper', THE WELL-
        WROUGHT URN (New York: Harcourt, Brace, 1947), in
        Killham (122) and Bloom (132)

        One of the first of the New Criticism attempts to show T as a
        poet of 'paradox, ambiguity, and ironic contrast'. In using
        'Tears, Idle Tears' Brooks was refuting F. R. Leavis's attack on
        the poem (138).

230   Stevenson, Lionel
        ' "The High-Born Maiden" Symbol in Tennyson', *PMLA*
        LXIII (1948) 234–43, in Killham (122)

        'Tennyson recurred to the image of an isolated and unhappy
        maiden with a persistence amounting almost to obsession.'
        With reference to 'The Lady of Shalott', 'The Palace of Art' and
        other early poems up to and including *The Princess*, this
        influential Jungian interpretation considers the development of
        the archetypal image of the *anima*, representing the uncon-
        scious, through three phases whereby T gains an emotional and
        artistic stability.

231   Hough, Graham
        ' "Tears, Idle Tears" ', *Hopkins Review* 4 (1951) 31–6, in
        Killham (122)

        An attempt to reassemble the poem after Brooks's dissection.
        Hough's contention is that the poem is not specific but is an
        associative evocation of 'undifferentiated regret and sorrow'
        for which Hallam's death and the memories prompted by a visit
        to Tintern Abbey, where the poem was written, were the
        trigger. A reply to Hough and a defence of Brooks's approach
        was provided by Leo Spitzer, ' "Tears, Idle Tears" Again',
        Hopkins Review 5 (1952) 71–80, also in Killham.

232   Stange, G. Robert
        'Tennyson's Garden of Art: A Study of "The Hesperides" ',
        PMLA LXVII (1952) 732–43, in Killham (122)

        An interpretation of T's symbolic presentation in 'The
        Hesperides' of 'the spiritual conditions under which the poetic
        experience comes to life'. Stange examines the Jungian motifs –

geological dualities, magic numbers, the island garden, and so on – and the subtle effects this symbolic patterning achieves. For an alternative reading, see Donna G. Fricke, 'Tennyson's "The Hesperides": East of Eden and Variations on the Theme', *TRB* (1970) 99–103; and, particularly, James D. Merriman, 'The Poet as Heroic Thief: Tennyson's "The Hesperides" Reexamined', *VN* 35 (1969) 1–5, who claims that 'The Hesperides' is 'a hard-headed examination of the moral evil, the psychological inadequacy and the pragmatic failure of retreat'.

233 Chiasson, E. J.
'Tennyson's "Ulysses" – A Re-interpretation', *UTQ* 23 (1954) 402–9, in Killham (122)

Summarises the debate on 'Ulysses' and contributes the view that the character of Ulysses is compounded of 'marital and social irresponsibility' in contrast to the virtues praised in Hallam in *In Memoriam*, with which 'Ulysses' is often linked.

234 Millhauser, Milton
'Tennyson's *Princess* and *Vestiges*', *PMLA* LXIX (1954) 337–43

In 1845, when T was writing the middle sections of *The Princess*, he read Chambers's *Vestiges of the Natural History of Creation* (1844) which seems to have been 'a precipitant but not a determinant' of T's ideas on geological history in the poem. This article is useful as a summary of the scientific movements of the time and on T's recoiling from full acceptance of their materialist implications.

235 Killham, John
TENNYSON AND *THE PRINCESS*: REFLECTIONS OF AN AGE (London: The Athlone Press, 1958)

This excellent book discusses developments in feminist and socialist thought during the two decades leading up to the publication of *The Princess* in 1847. The poem is then thoroughly investigated for its reflections of these ideas and for its other hybrid elements, such as echoes from T's reading of oriental poetry and theories about evolution. Killham's argument is that the 'strange form' of *The Princess* is a result of T's desire, under pressure from his critics, to give artistic expression to many of the urgent concerns of his time, particularly the 'woman question'.

236   Ryals, Clyde de L.
'The "Fatal Woman" Symbol in Tennyson', *PMLA* 74 (1959) 438–43

Inspired by Stevenson's Jungian analysis of the high-born maiden symbol in T's poetry (see 230), Ryals traces the influence of Keats's *femmes fatales* in poems such as 'Eleänore', suggesting that these dangerous women represent the 'sensual, morbid nature of [T's] romantic imagination'.

237   Pettigrew, John
'Tennyson's "Ulysses": A Reconciliation of Opposites', *VP* 1 (1963) 27–45

Summarises the criticism of this poem to date, traces many of the factors involved in its composition, such as the death of Hallam and the influence of Dante, and concludes that 'Ulysses' is the correlative not for one simple feeling but for a complexity of feelings: it is the 'unified product of a divided sensibility'.

238   Ryals, Clyde de L.
THEME AND SYMBOL IN TENNYSON'S POEMS TO 1850 (Philadelphia: University of Pennsylvania Press, 1964)

Described by the author as 'a handbook, of sorts' in that it moves through T's poetry poem by poem from 'Juvenilia' to *In Memoriam*, this takes the Nicolson view of T as an essentially introspective poet who struggled to reconcile his inner life with the social responsiveness required of a Victorian poet. Within these terms, Ryals argues clearly and persuasively and includes an unusually full and sympathetic section on *The Princess*.

239   Kissane, James
'Tennyson: The Passion of the Past and the Curse of Time', *ELH* 32 (1965) 85–109, in Francis (128)

A suggestive essay on the 'cleavage in consciousness' (resulting from what Spedding called T's 'almost personal dislike of the present') which is imaged in 'a disparity between the plenitude of external nature and the desolation of the conscious self . . . between *looking* on the happy autumn fields and *thinking* of the days that are no more'. The obsession with memory in T's poetry is a 'longing for a continuous present' which can both negate time and also intensify the sense of transience.

240   Rackin, Phyllis
        'Recent Misreadings of "Break, Break, Break" and Their Implications for Poetic Theory', *JEGP* 65 (1966) 217–28

Rackin argues that the simplicity of this lyric has confounded poetic theorists; in particular, she has Cleanth Brooks's *The Well-Wrought Urn* in mind in which 'the demand for paradox and striking metaphor obscure our vision of poems that work in other ways'.

241   Sendry, Joseph
        ' "The Palace of Art" Revisited', *VP* 4 (1966) 149–62

Argues that the poem's outcome is intimated in the description of the palace long before the apparently abrupt transition to the moral awareness of the last two stanzas.

242   Short, Clarice
        'Tennyson and 'The Lover's Tale" ', *PMLA* LXXXII (1967) 78–84

Examines the equivocal evidence concerning the relation of 'The Lover's Tale' to Boccaccio's story and concludes that the first three parts, written by T 'in my nineteenth year', drew on no Italian source but were of a part with T's other youthful poems of guilt and anguish.

243   Ostriker, Alicia
        'The Three Modes in Tennyson's Prosody', *PMLA* LXXXII (1967) 237–84

'Corrects' Pyre's thesis that the young T was 'rashly anarchic' about prosody by claiming that from 1830 to 1842 he wrote in three modes ('irregular' or 'ode', 'stanzaic' and 'sustained') as deliberate 'prosodic many-mindedness' in preparation for the later variety of *In Memoriam* and *Maud*.

244   Fredeman, William E.
' "A Sign Betwixt the Meadow and the Cloud": The Ironic Apotheosis of Tennyson's "St. Simeon Stylites" ', *UTQ* 38 (1968–9) 69–83

A full and rich analysis of this 'study in isolation and concomitant dehumanization'. The poem is first and foremost a dramatic monologue and not, as some critics have maintained, a simple attack on asceticism. As the anatomy of a man who 'perverts the moral system of his world', it is T's first extended experiment with the phenomenon of madness.

245   Bergonzi, Bernard
'Feminism and Femininity in *The Princess*, THE MAJOR VICTORIAN POETS: RECONSIDERATIONS, ed. Isabel Armstrong (London: Routledge & Kegan Paul, 1969) 35–50

Bergonzi sees *The Princess* as T's most thoughtful poem; his perplexity and apprehension concerning the ideas he presents are the cause of the strange form the poem takes.

246   Duncan-Jones, Catherine
'A Note on Tennyson's "Claribel" ', *VP* 9 (1971) 348–50

Points out the literary ancestry of 'Claribel' and its shared Romantic usage with Keats's 'Isabella' of emotion transmitted through natural objects.

247   Shaw, W. David
'Tennyson's "Tithonus" and the Problem of Mortality', *PQ* 52 (1973) 274–85

Shaw sees the poem as a reconciliation between Romantic and Classical ideas, a meeting-point between 'Ulysses' and *In Memoriam*.

248 Collins, Winston
'*The Princess*: The Education of the Prince', *VP* 11 (1973) 285–94

Argues that the prince's growth into wisdom and manliness represents a more serious didactic and aesthetic purpose in the poem than has usually been recognised.

249 Robbins, Tony
'Tennyson's "Ulysses": The Significance of the Homeric and Dantesque Backgrounds', *VP* 11 (1973) 177–93

By allusion to the heroic resolution of Homer's Odysseus and, particularly, Dante's Ulisse, T's poems makes a statement of imaginative faith and courage: 'Out of melancholy, despair, the consciousness of loss, morbid madness, rises faith, and with it the will to live'. For a recent, more wide-ranging study of T's poetry in relation to its sources, see Kenneth M. McKay, *Many Glancing Colours: An Essay in Reading Tennyson, 1809–1850* (Toronto: University of Toronto, 1988).

250 Bloom, Harold
'Tennyson: In the Shadow of Keats', POETRY AND REPRESSION: REVISIONISM FROM BLAKE TO STEVENS (New Haven and London: Yale UP, 1976) 143–74, in Bloom (132) and Francis (128)

'Anxiety of influence' in relation to T and his 'revisionist genius for internalizing Keats': a provocative discussion of T as 'one of the most sublimely repressed poets in the language' and 'Mariana' as 'a work genuinely alarming in its deepest implications'; it is a poem of 'belatedness', both erotic and poetic.

251 Gallant, Christine
'Tennyson's Use of the Nature Goddess in "The Hesperides", "Tithonus" and "Demeter and Persephone" ', *VP* 14 (1976) 155–60

Classical goddesses have a fascination for T all through his poetry; these are chthonian rather than Olympian, fertility figures possessing a cyclical, passive view of life which implicitly emphasises the dialectical nature of existence.

252   Welch, James Donald
       'Tennyson's Landscapes of Time and a Reading of "The
       Kraken" ', *VP* 14 (1976) 197–204

       This examines the two modes of time central to T's imagination,
       'the repetitive or static . . . usually associated with isolation'
       and the dynamic, purposeful and social; 'The Kraken' illus-
       trates both modes.

253   Eagleton, Terry
       'Tennyson: Politics and Sexuality in *The Princess* and *In
       Memoriam*', 1848: THE SOCIOLOGY OF LITERATURE,
       ed. Francis Barker *et al*. (Colchester: University of Essex,
       1978) 77–106

       A clever, provocative Lacanian interpretation of the two poems
       which sees them as registering great anxiety about patriarchal
       hegemony and subjectivity.

254   Lerner, Laurence
       'An Essay on *The Princess*', THE VICTORIANS, ed.
       Laurence Lerner (London: Methuen, 1978) 209–22

       Lucidly argues that T's feminism is at odds with his poetic
       sensibility; Ida's rejection of conventional femininity con-
       stitutes a rejection of lyric poetry.

255   Wickens, G. G.
       'The Two Sides of Early Victorian Science and the Unity of
       The Princess', *VS* 23 (1980) 369–88

       Wickens argues that the structural unity of *The Princess* de-
       pends on a 'distinction between . . . two sides of science': a
       bright side which 'maintains a teleology (and usually a theology
       as well) while considering the evidence of destruction and
       change in the material world – and a dark side of science' which
       mechanistically annotates the phenomena of change. This is an
       ingenious essay but one which ignores, or translates into its own
       terms, the sexual politics of the poem.

256   Mattheisen, Paul F.
       'Tennyson and Carlyle: A Source for "The Eagle" ', *VN* 60
       (1981) 1–3

This makes a convincing claim that 'The Eagle' is reminiscent of a passage from Carlyle's *Sartor Resartus* and that T shared with Carlyle a sense of the symbolic significance of the world of objects in which can be discerned, in Carlyle's terms, 'Eternity looking through Time'. For a recent study of them jointly as representative Victorian thinkers, see Michael Timko, *Carlyle and Tennyson* (London: Macmillan, 1988).

257   Pollard, Arthur
       'Three Horace Translations by Tennyson', *TRB* (1982) 16–24

T's early struggles with Horace, which he claimed spoilt the Latin poet for him, did not prevent him from making a competent translation of three of Horace's poems (Epode 5 and Odes I.9 and III.3) in his copy of Horace's *Odes* (now in TRC). Pollard compares these youthful translations with their originals.

258   Tucker, Herbert F.
       'Tennyson's Narrative of Desire: *'The Lover's Tale''* ', *VN* 62 (1982) 21–30

T's enduring obsession with this early, and for many years unpublished, work is explained as a way of investigating 'the relationship between a central self and other selves' which was a major preoccupation throughout his life.

259   Stevenson, Catherine Barnes
       'The Shade of Homer Exorcises the Ghost of De Quincey: Tennyson's 'The Lotos-Eaters'' ', *BIS* 10 (1982) 117–41

A painstaking account of T's response to the actualities of opium-eating (*via* his father and brother Charles) and to the Romantic mythology about opium which associated the drug with artistic creativity. Stevenson argues that the revisions T made to the poem show him distancing himself from the irresponsibility of the mariners.

260   Day, Aidan
       'The Spirit of Fable: Arthur Hallam and Romantic Values in Tennyson's "Timbuctoo"' ', *TRB* (1983) 59–71

The revisions T made to 'Armageddon' to transform it into 'Timbuctoo' suggest the degree of influence Hallam had on T's conceptions of poetry at this time. Day concludes that T adopted the Romantic ideology Hallam proposed but did so ambivalently and with reservations.

261   Joseph, Gerhard
'Tennyson's Stupidity', *University of Hartford Studies in Literature* 15 (1983) 55–62

An interesting psychoanalytic reading of 'Tears, Idle Tears' (and *In Memoriam*) which turns Auden's attack on T (88) as the 'stupidest' of the English poets to T's advantage by understanding ' "stupid" in its root sense of stunned, benumbed, or fixated by obscure early sorrow'. Joseph sees in the obsessive melancholy of T's poems a deep understanding of 'the mysteries of human sorrow . . . arguably one of the most profound [subjects] that poetry can explore'.

262   Boyd, John D. and Williams, Anne
'Tennyson's "Mariana" and "Lyric Perspective" ', *Studies in English Literature 1500–1900* 23 (1983) 579–93

Laboriously makes the worthwhile argument that the element called 'point of view' in prose fiction may be profitably emphasised in lyric poetry. 'Mariana', as a third person lyric, is a 'paradoxical blend of stasis and motion' in which the reader is also paradoxically stationed 'within and without', subject to shifting points of view.

263   Peltason, Timothy
'Supposed Confessions, Uttered Thoughts: The First Person Singular in Tennyson's Poetry', *VN* 64 (1983) 13–18

A comparison of 'Supposed Confessions' and 'Break, Break, Break' as admissions of 'the sad incompetence of human speech' to meet the expressive needs of the bereft and isolated self.

264   Peltason, Timothy
'Tennyson's Philosophy: Some Lyric Examples',
PHILOSOPHICAL APPROACHES TO LITERATURE:
NEW ESSAYS ON NINETEENTH AND TWENTIETH-
CENTURY TEXTS, ed. William E. Cain (Lewisburg:
Bucknell UP; London and Toronto: Associated UP, 1984)

A suggestively argued account of 'Tears, Idle Tears', 'Ulysses' and 'Tithonus' as philosophical poems using Heidegger's categorisation of mood as a way of describing 'the basic way in which we are *outside* ourselves. But that is the way we are essentially and constantly.' All three poems are concerned with the relationship of consciousness to time: 'Tears, Idle Tears' with the question of the presence of absence, 'Ulysses' with the expansion of a moment of consciousness into past and present, and 'Tithonus' as an immobilisation of consciousness in relationship to past and present.

265   Peltason, Timothy
       'Tennyson, Nature, and Romantic Nature Poetry', *PQ* 63 (1984) 75–93

A post-structuralist reading of 'The Dying Swan' as a modern development of the Romantic dialectic between the imagination and nature. T's poetry denies reciprocity between man and nature, subordinating the structures of nature to consciousness while also, in the absence of first person narratives, obliterating the self as an originator of conscious thought.

266   Johnson, Eileen Tess
       ' "This *Were* a Medley": Tennyson's *The Princess*', *ELH* 51 (1984) 549–74

The originality and brilliance of *The Princess* lies in its medley blend of 'variety, inclusiveness, energy, receptivity, and harmonious order' and in the 'heterogeneous mixture' of its literary styles – fairy story, romance, comedy, and ironic exposure of Romantic notions – which reflects its theme of sexual 'like in difference'.

267   Tucker, Herbert F.
       'From Monomania to Monologue: 'St. Simeon Stylites'' and the Rise of the Victorian Dramatic Monologue', *VP* 22 (1984) 121–37

'St. Simeon Stylites' is 'an exemplary monologue' in which the self is placed 'in context and thus into question'. This poem is considered in relation to T's other early monologues – 'Ulysses', 'Tithonus', 'Tiresias' – in which a reverse process occurs: the self attempts to excape from contexts in order to reclaim the transcendental.

268   Hilton, Nelson
       'Tennyson's "Tears": Idle, Idol, Idyl', *EC* 35 (1985) 223–37

       'Identity of semes makes for plurality of themes': an ingenious,
       playful, deconstructive explication of, primarily, 'Tears, Idle
       Tears'.

269   Ward, Geoffrey
       'Dying to Write: Maurice Planchot and Tennyson's
       "Tithonus" ', *Critical Inquiry* 12 (1985–6) 672–87

       An intriguing meditation on suicide and the 'human will to die'
       in 'Tithonus' and Planchot's *The Space of Literature* (1982).

270   Chadwick, Joseph
       'A Blessing and a Curse: The Poetics of Privacy in
       Tennyson's "The Lady of Shalott" ', *VP* 24 (1986) 13–30

       Chadwick argues that the Lady represents the Romantic no-
       tion, as expounded by Arthur Hallam, of the autonomy and
       femininity of the work of art, a notion deriving from a society
       radically split into private and public domains. Women, artists
       and art objects belong to the private sphere.

271   Harris, Daniel A.
       TENNYSON AND PERSONIFICATION: THE
       RHETORIC OF 'TITHONUS' (Michigan: Ann Arbor,
       1986)

       A difficult, learned, obscure, at times illuminating and provoca-
       tive study of T's use, particularly in 'Tithonus', of two types of
       prosopopoeia: the 'embodying and animating of abstractions'
       (which Tithonus does) and the 'imitative forgery' whereby a
       character's speech is impersonated. The tensions between the
       two kinds of personification (Tithonus's and T's) provide Harris
       with his theme.

272   Stone, Marjorie
       'Genre Subversion and Gender Inversion: *The Princess* and
       Aurora Leigh', *VP* 25 (1987) 101–27

In both poems the subversion of genre differences facilitates the questioning of gender distinctions; Barrett Browning is more radical than T in unsettling conventional genre and gender distinctions.

273   Edmond, Rod
' "A sweet disorder in the dresse": Tennyson's *The Princess*', AFFAIRS OF THE HEART (London and New York: Routledge, 1988) 90–129

Subtitled 'Victorian poetry and domestic narrative', this approachable study is concerned with the ideology of the middle-class family as it is articulated in five poems: Clough's *The Bothie of Toper-na-Fuosich*, T's *The Princess*, Elizabeth Barrett Browning's *Aurora Leigh*, Christina Rossetti's *Goblin Market* and Meredith's *Modern Love*. *The Princess* is seen as a contradictory text which is alert and sympathetic to contemporary feminism and the softening of gender categories, while endorsing the regulating structures of patriarchal marriage arrangements.

Criticism of Individual Poems

In Memoriam

Arthur Henry Hallam died in September 1833. During the next seventeen years Tennyson composed 'elegies' on his death which were arranged together and published as *In Memoriam* in June 1850. *In Memoriam* was published anonymously but the identity of the author was announced the same day in an advertisement in the *Publisher's Circular*. There had been a Trial edition of the poem privately issued in March of the same year; this had no title-page. The first edition added ten sections, plus further stanzas to section 124, to the Trial edition, bringing the number of sections to 129. Section 59 was added in the fourth edition in 1851 and section 39 was added in 1870. This brought the final total to 131 sections, plus the 'Prologue' and the Epilogue. *In Memoriam* was immediately successful, going to five editions by 1851. For an account of the composition of the poem, see Shatto and Shaw (94).

274   Gatty, Alfred
      A KEY TO TENNYSON'S *IN MEMORIAM* (London: George Bell, 1881)

      A section-by-section 'translation' of the poem 'to be consulted when the original puzzles the reader's mind'. T annotated a copy of the 'new and revised edition' of 1882 (TRC) and apparently took account of some of Gatty's remarks in his comments in Eversley.

275   Genung, John F.
      TENNYSON'S *IN MEMORIAM*: ITS PURPOSE AND ITS STRUCTURE (New York: Houghton Mifflin; Cambridge: Riverside Press, 1884)

      One of the earliest attempts to define its structure, this study notes the three Christmas-tides and the two and a half year internal time-span of the poem, and divides it into an Introductory Stage (sections 1–27), a First Cycle (28–77), a Second

Cycle (78–103), a Third Cycle (104–131) and a Concluding Invocation. The cycles correspond to the Past, Present and Future. Genung also makes interesting comparisons of the poem with 'Lycidas', 'Adonais' and Shakespeare's Sonnets.

276　Chapman, Elizabeth Rachel
A COMPANION TO *IN MEMORIAM* (London and New York: Macmillan, 1888)

Another section-by-section 'translation'.

277　Bradley, A. C.
A COMMENTARY ON TENNYSON'S *IN MEMORIAM* (London: Macmillan, 1901)

This is still the best guide to *In Memoriam*. Bradley's aim is to show 'the bearing of the sections on one another' and explain difficulties of interpretation. He professes to abstain from 'aesthetic criticism' but his introduction and his comments on parallel passages, metrical features and literary echoes, as well as his explications, provide valuable critical insights. He adheres to T's description of the structure of the poem as governed by the divisions made by the three Christmas-tides; within these four divisions, Bradley groups the sections according to narrative coherence or thematic similarity.

278　Eliot, T. S.
'Tennyson's *In Memoriam*', ESSAYS ANCIENT AND MODERN (London: Faber and Faber, 1936) 175–90. Reissued in SELECTED PROSE, ed. John Harward (London: Penguin, 1953) 176–85, in Hunt (290) and Killham (122)

Another famous essay, full of quotable comments, in which Eliot maintains that T is a great poet because 'he has three qualities which are seldom found together except in the greatest poets: abundance, variety, and complete competence'. *In Memoriam* 'is a long poem made by putting together lyrics, which have only the unity and continuity of a diary, the concentrated diary of a man confessing himself. It is a diary of which we have to read every word.' 'Its faith is a poor thing, but its doubt is a very intense experience. *In Memoriam* is a poem of despair, but of despair of a religious kind.'

279   Hough, Graham
'The Natural Theology of *In Memoriam*', *RES* XXIII (1947) 244–56, in Hunt (290)

An important essay which charts the change in religious apologetics from eighteenth-century reliance on natural analogy to a mid-nineteenth-century conviction that 'nature cannot lead men to God'. In *In Memoriam* T was trying to make a synthesis of the scientific thought of his age, particularly Lyell's *Principles of Geology*, and the transcendentalist ideas of Coleridge; the attempt was prompted and sustained by T's strong personal conviction and an 'unanalysable but completely cogent mystical experience'.

280   Mattes, Eleanor Bustin
IN MEMORIAM, THE WAY OF A SOUL: A STUDY OF SOME INFLUENCES THAT SHAPED TENNYSON'S POEM (New York: Exposition Press, 1951)

One of the first to suggest a tentative chronology for the composition of the sections of *In Memoriam*, Mattes also relates the development of the poem to T's personal circumstances and his reading of the work of predecessors and contemporaries such as Wordsworth, Isaac Taylor, Lyell, Robert Chambers, Herschel and Carlyle.

281   House, Humphry
'*In Memoriam*', ALL IN DUE TIME (London: Rupert Hart-Davies, 1955) 130–9

Originally a Third Programme talk in 1950, this argues that in the absence of a fixed faith, the Victorians turned for comfort and reassurance to an intensification of personal relationships. *In Memoriam* shows the '*fostering* of an affection' after Hallam's death in proportion to the increase in disturbing speculation about human life that his death caused.

282   Willey, Basil
        'Tennyson', MORE NINETEENTH CENTURY STUDIES
        (London: Chatto & Windus, 1956) 53–105

        Willey places T in 'A Group of Honest Doubters' and sees him
        as a representative sage caught between science and religion,
        faith and doubt. This essay is mainly on *In Memoriam*, which is
        'not a distinctively Christian poem' and which Willey admires as
        'a long poem free from epic pomp, and built up, like a coral
        reef, entirely from living organisms'.

283   Johnson, E. D. H.
        'The Way of the Poet', *VS* II (1958) 139–48, in Hunt (290)

        Discusses T's artistic development from 1833 to 1850 as regis-
        tered in the progress through four stages of the poet-figure in *In
        Memoriam* from a notion of poetry as therapy to the belief in it
        as a mission.

284   Svaglic, Martin J.
        'A Framework for Tennyson's *In Memoriam*', *JEGP* LXI
        (1962) 810–25

        In 'Aspects of Tennyson II' (*Nineteenth Century* XXXIII, 1893)
        (see 2), Knowles reported T as saying that 'there were nine
        natural groups or divisions in the Poem, as follows: from Stanza
        I to Stanza VIII; from IX to XX; from XXI to XXVII; from
        XXVIII to XLIX; from L to LVIII; from LIX to LXXI; from
        LXXII to XCVIII; from XCIX to CIII; from CIV to CXXXI'.
        Svaglic offers a reading based on this scheme to provide a
        rationale of the poem as a treatise on the Platonic idea that 'men
        may rise on stepping-stones / Of their dead selves to higher
        things'.

285   Mays, J. C. C.
        '*In Memoriam*: An Aspect of Form', *UTQ* 35 (1965–6) 22–
        46, in Hunt (290)

        In *In Memoriam* T accepted the necessity of form as an expres-
        sion of spirit, and the working out of form in the poem is
        'founded upon tension and opposition even if towards the close
        of the poem it is opposition largely reconciled'. Mays's import-
        ant essay demonstrates the varying ways in which the recurring

pattern of opposition is stated, 'so the whole progression of the poem is through opposition playing against itself . . . in a kind of decreasing undulating movement'.

286   Sendry, Joseph
    '*In Memoriam* and *Lycidas*', *PMLA* 82 (1967) 437–43

T admired *Lycidas* as 'a test of any reader's poetic instinct', and Sendry discerns thematic echoes in *In Memoriam*: the sea voyage (sections 9–16), nostalgia for youthful academe (22–6), and the debate on fame (73–7). Like *Lycidas*, *In Memoriam* also makes an apologetic intrusion of philosophic elements into the elegiac pattern.

287   August, Eugene, R.
    'Tennyson and Teilhard: The Faith of *In Memoriam*', *PMLA* 84 (1969) 217–26

Argues that the faith of *In Memoriam* is 'radically modern' and foreshadows a dynamic strand of twentieth-century religious thought best expressed by Teilhard de Chardin in his concern with 'faith beyond the forms of faith' and the process of 'Christogenesis' throughout the universe. T and Teilhard also share persuasive rather than dogmatic styles of writing.

288   Millhauser, Milton
    'Tennyson, *Vestiges*, and the Dark Side of Science', *VN* 35 (Spring 1969) 22–5

T bought a copy of Robert Chambers's *Vestiges of Natural Creation* in 1844, very soon after it was published. Section 118 and the Epilogue of *In Memoriam* were probably influenced by Chambers's cosmological ideas, and sections 120 and 122–4, which deny science and try to rise above it, may have been affected by the negative reviews *Vestiges* received.

289   Hirsch, Gordon D.
    'Tennyson's *Commedia*', *VP* 8 (1970) 93–106

The influence of Dante and the Dantean tradition on *In Memoriam* is evidenced in borrowings, analogues, allusions and in the concluding symbolic marriage but T personalises this model, particularly in his rapport with the Beatrice figure of Hallam.

290 Hunt, John Dixon (ed.)
TENNYSON: IN MEMORIAM (London: Macmillan (Casebook Series), 1970)

A very useful collection of essays in three sections: (i) 'Two Essays by Arthur Hallam' (from 'Theodicaea Novissima' (41) and from 'On Some of the Characteristics of Modern Poetry' (220)); (ii) 'Victorian Reviews and Reactions' (J. Westland Marston; G. H. Lewes; *North British Review*; Franklin Lushington; *The English Review*; *The Times*; F. W. Robertson; Henry Sidgwick); and (iii) 'Modern Criticism' (T. S. Eliot: '*In Memoriam*' (278)); Graham Hough: 'The Natural Theology of *In Memoriam*' (279); Arthur J. Carr: 'Tennyson as a Modern Poet' (139); Humphry House: 'Poetry and Philosophy in *In Memoriam*'; Walker Gibson: 'Behind the Veil; A Distinction Between Poetic and Scientific Language in Tennyson, Lyell, and Darwin'; E. D. H. Johnson: 'The Way of the Poet' (283); John D. Rosenberg: 'The Two Kingdoms of *In Memoriam*'; Jerome H. Buckley: 'The Way of the Soul'; Jonathon Bishop: 'The Unity of *In Memoriam*'; Carlisle Moore: 'Faith, Doubt and Mystical Experience';
J. C. C. Mays: '*In Memoriam*: An Aspect of Form' (285)

291 Hunt, John Dixon
'The Symbolist Vision of *In Memoriam*', *VP* 8 (1970) 187–98

In its use of dream, trance and 'musical' suggestion, and in its acceptance of noumenal rather than phenomenal vision, *In Memoriam* may be seen as an early symbolist poem.

292 Langbaum, Robert
'The Dynamic Unity of *In Memoriam*', THE MODERN SPIRIT (London: Chatto & Windus, 1970) 51–75, in Bloom (132)

Langbaum's argument is that we do not value *In Memoriam* for its ponderings on faith and science but for the epistemological sophistication which unifies the disparate intellectual elements in the poem. Langbaum maintains that *In Memoriam* hinges on section 95 when a total transformation of perception occurs: 'All the old facts and problems are transvaluated and absorbed into the affirmative movement' that dominates from this section to the end of the poem.

293   Sinfield, Alan
THE LANGUAGE OF TENNYSON'S *IN MEMORIAM*
(Oxford: Basil Blackwell, 1971)

This is a densely argued, rewarding study, in which close textual analysis is informed by a knowledge of linguistics. Its premiss is that the poetic significance of *In Memoriam* lies in 'a structure and language [which] are the product of a desperate need for order in the absence of any clear and agreed means of establishing it'. The diction, syntax, imagery and rhythm of the poem, and their interrelationships, are examined with a view to present-day responses and also in the context of the main currents of thought of the nineteenth and twentieth centuries. Sinfield writes with elegance and sensitivity on the details of the poem and communicates his enthusiasm for its greatness.

294   Boyd, John D.
'*In Memoriam* and the "Logic of Feeling" ', *VP* 10 (1972) 95–110

By 'logic of feeling' (Oliver Elton's phrase) is meant the psychological responses of a single human sensibility 'whose experience *is* the whole of the poem'. These responses may conflict with empirical or scientific logic but structure the argument nevertheless; they are particularly manifest in T's use of landscape description.

295   Mason, Michael Y.
'*In Memoriam*: The Dramatization of Sorrow', *VP* 10 (1972) 161–77

A complex, at times difficult, but insightful discussion of the effects T achieves through a sophisticated use of pathetic fallacy by which he structures and dramatises the development of the mourner in the poem from weakness to strength and assurance: 'a kind of encoding of attitudes into features of lyrical poetry takes place'.

296   Niermeier, Stuart F. C.
        '*In Memoriam* and *The Excursion*: A Matter of Comparison',
        VN 41 (1972) 20–2

        On Wordsworth's influence on T.

297   Sendry, Joseph
        'Tennyson's "Butcher's Books" as Aids to Composition', *VP*
        11 (1973) 55–9

        An important article making use of the Lincoln MS of *In
        Memoriam* as well as the Trinity MS and other sources to
        speculate on T's methods and progress in the composition of *In
        Memoriam* and the 'distinct help' the long ledger-type butcher's
        books were in organising the poem.

298   McSweeney, Kerry
        'The Pattern of Natural Consolation in *In Memoriam*', *VP* 11
        (1973) 87–99

        With particular reference to section 95 McSweeney examines
        the pattern of pastoral elegy in *In Memoriam* and the poem's
        discovery of a natural, cyclic acceptance of life and death which
        is consoling but somewhat at odds with a Christian affirmation
        of an after-life.

299   Gliserman, Susan
        'Early Victorian Science Writers and Tennyson's *In
        Memoriam*: A Study in Cultural Exchange', *VS* 18 (1975)
        277–308, 437–59

        This two-part article documents T's debt in *In Memoriam* to the
        rhetoric of the early Victorian science writers and the debt
        science came to owe to him for the part his poem played in
        familiarising scientific ideas.

300   Laird, Robert G
        'Tennyson and "The Bar of Michael Angelo": A Possible
        Source for *In Memoriam* LXXXVII.40', *VP* 14 (1976) 253–5

        The suggested source is George Combe's *A System of Phrenol-
        ogy* (1825 and 1830; two-volume edition 1843) which described

the brow as the organ of individuality and commented that it appeared as exceptionally large in the portraits of Michelangelo.

301   Sinfield, Alan
' "That Which Is": The Platonic Indicative of *In Memoriam* XCV', *VP* 14 (1976) 247–52

A densely argued discussion of the tradition of religious and mystical thought behind line 39 of Section 95 and T's use of the indicative – among so much of the subjunctive – to confirm, even if only momentarily, an apprehension of absolute reality.

302   Kennedy, Ian H.C.
'*In Memoriam* and the Tradition of Pastoral Elegy', *VP* 15 (1977) 351–66

T's practice is to exploit the pastoral conventions while at the same time questioning their validity.

303   Shaw, Marion
'*In Memoriam* and Popular Religious Poetry', *VP* 15 (1977) 1–8

In form, imagery and expressions of faith and doubt, *In Memoriam* echoes hymns of the eighteenth and early nineteenth centuries to exploit the familiar devotional responses of its readers.

304   Waller, John O.
'Francis Turner Palgrave's Criticisms of Tennyson's *In Memoriam*', *VN* 52 (Fall 1977) 13–17

Palgrave's annotated copy of *In Memoriam* (TRC) was intended to be read by T, who may have made 'at most two or three minor revisions' in the edition of 1855 in response to Palgrave's annotations. See also Marion Shaw, 'Palgrave's *In Memoriam*', *VP* 18 (1980) 199–201.

305   Shatto, Susan
'Tennyson's Revisions of *In Memorium*', *VP* 16 (1978) 341–56

This focuses on heavily revised sections – 31, 32, 59, 123, 124, 128 and 130 – and compares versions in the manuscripts, the Trial edition and the early editions and concludes that although the differences are on the whole slight, there is the notable feature of a progressive depersonalisation of references to Hallam and to the poet himself.

306   Sendry, Joseph
       '*In Memoriam*: Twentieth Century Criticism', *VP* 18 (1980) 105–18

This is the first article in a special issue of *Victorian Poetry* devoted exclusively to *In Memoriam*. The other articles are: Dolores Ryback Rosenblum, 'The Act of Writing *In Memoriam*' (307); Richard J. Dunn, 'Vision and Revision: *In Memoriam* XCV'; Peter Allan Dale, ' "Gracious Lies": The Meaning of Metaphor in *In Memoriam*'; Dennis M. Welch, 'Distance and Progress in *In Memoriam*'; Robert Dilligan, 'Computers and Style: The Prososdy of *In Memoriam*' (308); Marion Shaw, 'Palgrave's *In Memoriam*'; Christopher P. Baker, 'Milton's Nativity Ode and *In Memoriam* CVI'. Sendry's review of criticism, which begins with Bradley's *Commentary* (277), particularly commends Hough (279), Sinfield (293), and the relevant chapters in Buckley (121), Priestley (211) and Pitt (123).

307   Rosenblum, Dolores Ryback
       'The Act of Writing *In Memoriam*', *VP* 18 (1980) 119–34

T's obsession with the act of language, and its contrary impulses of introspection and expressive progression, is a cyclic structural principle in the poem. It can be seen as related to his lifelong preoccupation with dualisms, oppositions never satisfactorily resolved but providing language with its meaningful surfaces and depths.

308   Dilligan, Robert
       'Computers and Style: The Prosody of *In Memoriam*', *VP* 18 (1980) 179–96

A computational analysis which confirms Robert Langbaum's observation in 'The Dynamic Unity of *In Memoriam*' (292) that the poem has 'a dynamic unity of thought and feeling dependent on a dialectical principle of growth of a single consciousness'. Dilligan offers a defence of computational criticism and sees it as the shape of things to come.

309   Wordsworth, Ann
'An Art That Will Not Abandon the Self to Language: Bloom, Tennyson and the Blind World of the Wish', UNTYING THE TEXT, ed. Robert Young (Boston, London, Henley-on-Thames: Routledge & Kegan Paul, 1981) 207–22

More about Bloom than T but still an interesting application of Bloomian psychopoetics (which are contrasted with orthodox criticism) to T's 'beautiful and uneasy' poems of mourning, particularly *In Memoriam* and its triumph of the creative will over belatedness and death.

310   Armstrong, Isabel
'Tennyson, The Collapse of Object and Subject: *In Memoriam*', LANGUAGE AS LIVING FORM IN NINETEENTH CENTURY POETRY (Brighton: Harvester; Totowa, New Jersey: Barnes and Noble, 1982) 172–205

A subtle, complex and sometimes difficult post-structuralist account of nineteenth-century 'idealist' language which 'discloses a concern with the relationship of subject and object and the nature of reality'. *In Memoriam* displays 'a fundamental anxiety . . . about the dissolution of language altogether' but with great intelligence and courage 'repeatedly builds itself out of its collapse by giving full play to the language which threatens its destruction'.

311   Hinchcliffe, Peter
'Elegy and Epithalamium in *In Memoriam*', UTQ 52 (1982/3) 241–62

An intelligent and thoughtful essay which claims that the coherence of *In Memoriam* is rhetorical rather than argumentative or thematic and is provided by acceptance of the requirements of elegy. The generic change from elegy to epithalamium in the Epilogue attempts to resolve the 'impasse of anxiety' that T's elegiac formulations have created.

312 Manning, Sylvia
'Tennyson's Courtship of Sorrow', *VN* 67 (Spring 1985) 10–13

A perceptive psychoanalytic reading of *In Memoriam* as a love poem as much as an elegy because the act of grieving becomes entangled with the act of loving and the work of mourning is thereby arrested and prolonged.

313 Sacks, Peter M.
THE ENGLISH ELEGY: STUDIES IN THE GENRE
FROM SPENSER TO YEATS (Baltimore and London:
Johns Hopkins UP, 1985) 166–203

This includes a sophisticated, psychoanalytic and mythopoeic interpretation of *In Memoriam* which sees the prolonged accretion of its composition as necessary to sustain 'such a burden of skepticism and such a passionate clinging to the empirical and personal'.

314 Sinfield, Alan
'Tennyson's Strategies of Presence and the Idea of
Literature', POETRY AND EPISTEMOLOGY, ed. Roland
Hagenbuchle and Laura Skandera (Regensburg, Germany:
Freidrich Pustet, 1986)

An accessible attempt to give a political dimension to a post-structuralist reading of *In Memoriam*; Sinfield discusses the poem's unease at the adequacy and authenticity of language in communicating fullness of meaning in relation to the nineteenth-century construct of 'literature' and T's negotiations between the 'two alternatives for poetry in his time – incorporation and marginalization'.

315 Hirsh, Elizabeth A.
' "No Record of Reply"': *In Memoriam* and Victorian
Language Theory', *ELH* 55 (Spring 1988) 233–57

This makes a subtle and complex comparison between *In Memoriam* and a classic work of Anglican speculation, John Donaldson's *The New Cratylus* (1839). The crux of the intersection between the two works is 'the identification of writing as a form of artificial memory, inferior to organic/phonetic memory but still essential for the preservation and dissemination of the logos'.

Maud

Maud was published in 1855, Tennyson having composed it with unusual rapidity during the previous year. But the 'germ' of *Maud* was a lyric, 'Oh! That 'twere Possible', composed in 1833–4 soon after the death of Arthur Hallam, a version of which was published in *The Tribute* in 1837 as a favour to his friend Monckton Milnes. This lyric became *Maud* ii 141–238. For an account of the manuscripts and editions, see Shatto (95); for the background to the poem see Rader (11); and for its reception see Shannon (324).

316   [Aytoun, W. E.]
'Maud', *Blackwood's Magazine* 78 (September 1855) 311–21

An extreme example of the adverse criticism *Maud* received. Aytoun thought it showed T 'losing ground with each successive effort' and that it was an 'ill-conceived and worse-expressed screed of bombast'. He seems not to have realised that the poem is a monodrama.

317   [Kingsley, Charles]
'Maud', *Fraser's Magazine* 52 (1855) 264–73

Kingsley, who much admired *In Memoriam* (*Fraser's Magazine* 42 (1850) 245–55, in Jump (158)), was disappointed with *Maud* although he did think its study of madness served as a warning to the nation not to behave like the French and run mad *en masse*. He also thought the hero of *Maud* lacked manliness; although 'Come into the Garden' is unequalled as a lyric, 'will not the world say that it is now and then rather the passion of a Southern woman than of an English man?'

318   [Gladstone, W. E.]
[Review of] '*Maud and Other Poems*', *New Quarterly Review* 4 (1855) 393–7, in Jump (158)

Gladstone was later to modify his views but at this point he considered *Maud*, in spite of many beauties, to be a failure, primarily because of its 'catch-penny clap-trap' about the cleansing properties of war. Although he does not make the common mistake of confusing T with his hero, Gladstone nevertheless considers that the hero 'speaks too much to the pit'.

319   Mann, Robert James
TENNYSON'S *MAUD* VINDICATED: AN
EXPLANATORY ESSAY (London: Jarrold & Sons, 1856),
extract in Jump (158)

This is a careful defence of *Maud* against hostile criticism; it
summarises the plot and draws sympathetic attention to T's
psychological and technical skill. T was grateful to Mann: 'No
one with this essay before him can in future pretend to mis-
understand my dramatic poem "Maud": your commentary is as
true as it is full' (*Memoir* I 405).

320   Wolfe, Humbert
TENNYSON (Poets on Poets Series, No. 3) (London: Faber
& Faber, 1930)

One of the most adulatory inter-war attempts to rehabilitate T,
this brief hymn of praise to *Maud* describes it as the first
Modernist poem: 'When Mr. T. S. Eliot wrote *The Wasteland*
he was merely carrying the *Maud* scheme to an almost pain-
fully logical conclusion;. The comments of Wolfe, a poet himself, on the metrical virtuosities of *Maud* are particularly
interesting.

321   Howe, Merrill Levi
'Dante Gabriel Rossetti's Comments on *Maud*', *Modern
Language Notes* 49 (1934) 290–3

Howe annotates two unpublished letters to William Allingham
in which Rossetti, who disliked *Maud*, gives an amusing account of hearing T read *Maud* and rage against its reviewers.

322   Basler, Roy P.
'Tennyson's *Maud*', SEX, SYMBOLISM AND
PSYCHOLOGY IN LITERATURE (New Brunswick, New
Jersey: Rutgers UP, 1948) 73–93

A controversial and influential essay which claimed a Jungian
insight on T's part in the success of *Maud* as a study in 'psychic
frustration' and a poem which 'pioneered the uncharted front-
iers of psychological phenomena'.

323   Johnson, E. D. H.
       'The Lily and the Rose: Symbolic Meaning in Tennyson's
       Maud', *PMLA* 64 (1949) 1222–7

       One of the first essays to point out the dramatic interplay in
       Maud of the symbolic meanings of innocence and passion
       traditionally associated with lilies and roses. Still an illuminat-
       ing discussion, and interesting also in its alignment of T with the
       nineteenth-century *symboliste* movement.

324   Shannon, Edgar Finley
       'The Critical Reception of Tennyson's *Maud*', *PMLA* 68
       (1953) 397–417

       This continues from Shannon's book, *Tennyson and the Re-
       viewers* (1952) (156) and offers an authoritative account of T's
       most 'vehement effort as a social critic and reformer' and the
       dismay and bewilderment that greeted it. T had 'misjudged his
       audience and had projected his poetry too deeply into the
       realms of abnormal psychology, politics, and opinion'. Shan-
       non claims that T was influenced by the critics to the extent of
       making small alterations to the poem in subsequent editions.

325   Marshall, George O.
       'An Incident from Carlyle in Tennyson's *Maud*', *NQ* 6 (1959)
       77–8

       T's use of 'Mammonite mother' (I i 45) can be traced to Carlyle,
       especially Book ii of *Past and Present* which refers to parents
       killing their children for a burial fee.

326   Killham, John
       'Tennyson's *Maud* – The Function of the Imagery', in
       Killham (122) 219–35

       Killham's position is that imagery is as important in *Maud* as the
       themes and the characterisation, and proceeds to show how the
       poem is illuminated by animal, jewel and stone imagery, and by
       luxurious 'Persian' images.

327   Schweik, Robert C.
       'The "Peace or War" Passages in Tennyson's *Maud*', *NQ* 7
       (1960) 457–8

This argues convincingly that an article, 'Peace and War, A Dialogue', in *Blackwood's Edinburgh Magazine* LXXVI (November 1854), provided the source for the commitment to war of the hero of *Maud*. For corroboration of this argument, see C. Ricks, 'Peace and War and *Maud*', *NQ* n.s. 9 (1962) 230.

328   Truss, T. J.
'Tennysonian Aspects of *Maud*', *University of Mississippi Studies in English* 1 (1960) 105–17

Points out that many features of *Maud* which contemporary critics found shocking, were present in T's earlier work.

329   Rader, R. W.
'The Composition of Tennyson's *Maud*', *Modern Philology* 59 (1962) 165–9

The evidence Rader assembles leads him to suggest that T had thought about developing a long poem from 'Oh! That 'twere Possible' long before Sir John Simeon gave him the idea in 1855. See also 'Tennyson in the Year of Hallam's Death', *PLMA* 77 (1962) 419–24. Both articles are used in *Tennyson's Maud* (1963) (11).

330   Stokes, Edward
'The Metrics of *Maud*', *VP* 2 (1964) 97–110

A thorough investigation of the variety of versification in *Maud* and an illuminating attempt to show the dramatic appropriateness and effectiveness of the different metrical styles.

331   Ray, Gordon N.
'Tennyson Reads *Maud*', Sedgewick Memorial Lecture, 1968 (Vancouver: University of British Columbia Press, 1968)

Ray recounts how he purchased Vol. IV, containing *In Memoriam* and *Maud*, of the six-volume *edition de luxe* of T's *Works* published by Strahan & Co. in 1872. The volume contains annotations by Knowles, approved by T, based on readings and conversations during 1870–1. Most of T's comments on *In Memoriam* appeared in Knowles's memorial article in *Nineteenth Century* (see 2), but those on *Maud* have not been hitherto recorded. T's comments paraphrase the poem and explain the psychology of the narrator.

332   Byatt, A. S.
'The Lyric Structure of Tennyson's *Maud*', THE MAJOR VICTORIAN POETS, ed. Isabel Armstrong (London: Routledge & Kegan Paul, 1969) 69–92

A complex and thoughtful essay which argues that in *Maud* T makes use of the 'timeless and impersonal aspects of the lyric form' to chart the hero's growth towards maturity. Byatt suggests that the Victorians appreciated the 'formal complexity and general scope of *Maud* better than we have recently been able to do, paradoxically because they were better able to respond to . . . the value of *feeling* in the lyric and the value of immediate sensual response in description, rhythm and imagery'.

333   Chandler, Alice
'Tennyson's *Maud* and the Song of Songs', *VP* 7 (1969) 91–104

Points illuminatingly to parallels, particularly in Part I of *Maud* which can be seen, like the Song, as an allegory of the soul's love for God; in Part II the language is more like that of Revelation. The transition marks T's darkening vision, developed in *Idylls*.

334   Drew, Philip
'Tennyson and the Dramatic Monologue: A Study of *Maud*', in Palmer (125) 115–46

Drew argues trenchantly that although by comparison with Browning, T wrote 'no dramatic monologues worthy of the name', yet *Maud* as a monodrama is nevertheless a socially alert poem which, by means of masks, puts before its audience a 'series of investigations [into] the received attitudes [T] expressed so emphatically and memorably in his public poems'.

335   Mermin, Dorothy M.
'Tennyson's *Maud*: A Thematic Analysis', *TSLL* 15 (1973) 267–77

Argues lucidly that T, like Arnold, responded to pressure to be a poet of contemporary issues and that his growing acceptance of the present over an irrevocably lost past can be traced from 'Locksley Hall' to 'Enoch Arden'; in this context the decision of the hero of *Maud* to fight in the Crimean War should be judged positively, as a 'happy' ending which nevertheless is, perhaps, 'poetically a bad one'.

336   Wordsworth, Jonathan
' "What Is It, That Has Been Done?" ', The Central Problem of *Maud*', *EC* 24 (1974) 356–62

A provocative and exciting post-Freudian approach to *Maud* as a 'poem about sexual guilt and remorse' centred on two deaths: the hero's father and Maud's brother. Wordsworth thinks Part III 'by any standards, and, on any reading, a mistake'. For a rejoinder to Wordsworth, see Frank R. Giordano, 'The "Red Ribbed Hollow": Suicide and Part III in *Maud*', *NQ* 24 (1977) 402–4, who argues that Part III is the sublimation of the hero's suicidal impulses and the working out of Maud's martial song.

337   Spatz, Jonas
'Love and Death in Tennyson's *Maud*', *TSLL* 16 (1974) 503–10

Again in psychoanalytic vein, Spatz interprets the hero's love for Maud as a 'neurotic symptom', the result of repressed murderous instincts.

338   Kennedy, Ian H. C.
'The Crisis of Language in Tennyson's *Maud*', *TSLL* 9 (1977) 161–78

T's doubts about 'the capability of language truly to communicate at all' gain their fullest and most moving expression in *Maud*, in which the attempts to convey love fail and are overtaken by babble, and where a 'uncontrolled murderous mode of speech' finally prevails. Kennedy's analysis acknowledges T's conscious intentions in the poem while also allowing for a darker implicit meaning.

339   Hoge, James O.
'Jowett on Tennyson's *Maud*: A New Letter', *NQ* 24 (1977)
16–8

Jowett rushed to the defence of *Maud* when many were decrying it. His helpful letter to T of December 1855, reflecting upon the outcry and advising T how he should respond, is quoted here in full.

340   Kurata, Marilyn J.
' "A Juggle Born of the Brain": A new Reading of *Maud*',
VP 21 (1983) 369–78

Kurata's controversial case is that the speaker in *Maud* is self-deluded throughout and that there is no evidence that Maud ever returns his affection or exists at all. This and similar readings of the poem are objected to by Chris R. Vanden Bossche, 'Realism versus Romance: The War of Cultural Codes in Tennyson's *Maud*', *VP* 24 (1968) 69–82, who attempts to place the hero's bellicose attitudes in the context of contemporary utterances, particularly those of Ruskin.

341   Longy, Robert E.
'The Sound and Silence of Madness: Language as Theme in Tennyson's *Maud*', *VP* 22 (1984) 407–26

'We need to add Tennyson's name to Foucault's list [of nineteenth-century artists – Holderlin, Nerval, Nietzsche and Artand] in whose work the 'life of unreason" manifests itself.'

Idylls of the King

Idylls of the King, here given in the order of their final arrangement, were published as follows:

1862	Dedication [To the Prince Consort]	
1869	'The Coming of Arthur'	
1872	'Gareth and Lynette'	
1859	'The Marriage of Geraint'	originally published together as
1859	'Geraint and Enid'	'Enid', divided into two parts 1873, final titles 1886

1885 'Balin and Balan'
1859 'Merlin and Vivien'   originally published as 'Vivien', final
                                 title 1870
1859 'Lancelot and Elaine'   originally published as 'Elaine', final
                                 title 1870
1869 'The Holy Grail'
1869 'Pelleas and Ettarre'
1871 'The Last Tournament'
1859 'Guinevere'
1869 'The Passing of Arthur'
1873 'To the Queen'

For an account of the manuscripts and editions, see Pfordresher (93); for the serial evolution and background to the poem, see Gray (378).

342   [Bagehot, Walter]
      'Tennyson's *Idylls*', *National Review* IX (October 1859) 368–
      94, in Jump (158)

      Bagehot records T's general popularity: 'Everybody admires
      Tennyson now: but to admire him fifteen years ago was to be a
      Tennysonian'. Bagehot did not like *Maud* and finds *Idylls* a
      refreshing contrast. In his view, T is not an original thinker but a
      'first rate *realiser* and realisation is a test of truth'.

343   [Gladstone, William Ewart]
      'Tennyson's Poem – *Idylls of the King*', *Quarterly Review*
      CVI (October 1859) 454–85, in Jump (158)

      This is Gladstone's most positive review of T's poetry (he had
      not liked *Maud*). He approves of the 'higher conception of the
      nature of women' in *Idylls*, of T's 'extraordinary felicity and
      force in the use of metaphor and simile', and his grasp of 'the
      genuine law which makes man and not the acts of men the base
      of epic song'.

344   Ludlow, J. M.
      'Moral Aspects of Mr. Tennyson's *Idylls of the King*',
      Macmillan's Magazine I (November 1859) 64–72

      A sympathetic review from a Christian Socialist who approves
      of the poem's emphasis on 'Reformation through love',

although he regrets that T has given the impression that 'the self-righteous Arthur is his ideal of manliness'.

345   Alford, Henry
[Review of 'Last Tournament', 'Pelleas and Ettarre', 'The Coming of Arthur', and 'The Passing of Arthur'],
Contemporary Review 13 (1870) 104–27

Alford, who had known T at Cambridge, is one of the first critics to note the overall allegorical drift of the sequence; he comments on a conflict in the poem 'continually maintained between the spirit and the flesh'. According to Hallam Tennyson, T considered this review, and the one by J. T. Knowles (347), to be the best, although later he complained that critics had 'explained some things too allegorically, although there is an allegorical or perhaps parabolic drift in the poem' (notes to Eversley edition).

346   Swinburne, Algernon Charles
UNDER THE MICROSCOPE (London: D. White, 1872)
36–45

T features in this provocative pamphlet by one of the earliest and most vociferous of his detractors, and also one of the most admiring. Swinburne is particularly hostile to *Idylls of the King* which he calls 'The Morte d'Albert'. He believes T has degraded the Arthurian story to 'a case for the divorce court', with Arthur a 'wittol', Guinevere 'a woman of intrigue' and Lancelot the 'correspondent'. These points were made more restrainedly in Swinburne's 'Tennyson and Musset', *Fortnightly Review* 35 (1881) 129–53. For an account of the relationship between T and Swinburne, see Kerry McSweeney, 'Swinburne's Tennyson', *VS* 22 (1978) 5–28.

347   Knowles, James T.
'The Meaning of Mr. Tennyson's "King Arthur" ',
Contemporary Review 21 (May 1873) 938–48

Knowles had already written a letter on 'The Holy Grail' to the *Spectator* 43 (January 1870) 15–17 (in Jump (158)), having been encouraged to do so by T 'upon the lines he himself indicated. He often said, however, that an allegory should never be pressed too far' (*Memoir* II.126 fn.). Knowles develops his earlier view of *Idylls* as a unified work describing 'the soul in its war with sense'.

348 Littledale, H.
ESSAYS ON LORD TENNYSON'S *IDYLLS OF THE KING* (London: Macmillan, 1893)

A careful study, consisting mostly of extended notes comparing *Idylls* with source material, primarily Malory but also Lady Charlotte Guest's translation of the *Mabinogion*. Littledale's is one of the more useful to the modern reader of nineteenth-century studies. See also George D. Meinhold, '*Idylls of the King* and the *Mabinogion*'. *TRB* (1969).

349 Cross, T. P.
'Alfred Tennyson as a Celticist', *Modern Philology* 18 (1921) 485–92

A well-researched article which argues that T believed in the historical Arthur and 'made an honest attempt to ground his *Idylls* in the most reputable authorities of his day'.

350 Boas, F. S.
'Tennyson and the Arthurian Legend', FROM RICHARDSON TO PINERO (London: John Murray, 1936) 210–29

Writing at the height of anti-Victorianism, and therefore at a time when T's most Victorian poem was in greatest disrepute, Boas defends *Idylls*; it may fail as an organic whole but it does have a 'strangely fitful inspiration'.

351 Priestley, F. E. L.
'Tennyson's *Idylls*', *UTQ* 19 (1949) 35–49, in Killham (122)

In this influential post-war essay Priestley became one of the first to argue for the philosophical integrity of *Idylls* against criticism of it as ornate escapism. *Idylls* enforces 'the validity and necessity of idealism' to counter materialism and hedonism, and the poem's contention is that 'it is of the essence of ethics to be not descriptive but normative'.

352   Burchell, Samuel C.
'Tennyson's "Allegory in the Distance" ', *PMLA* 68 (1953)
418–24

The phrase is Jowett's and Burchell uses it to argue for the
suggestiveness of *Idylls*; it is 'not rooted in one dogmatic
principle of Soul versus Body, but [is] a medley of pure and
symbolic narrative – a revelation, a diagnosis'. Burchell's article is a defence of *Idylls* against another hostile contemporary
attitude, that it is simple Victorian moralising.

353   Engelberg, Edward
'The Beast Image in Tennyson's *Idylls of the King*', *ELH* 22
(1955) 287–92

Engelberg shows by example how Arthur's kingdom 'reels back
into the beast' and argues that the recurrence of beast images
gives the work unity and dramatic intensity. One of the first of
many such studies.

354   Miller, Betty
'Tennyson and the Sinful Queen', *Twentieth Century* 158
(October 1955) 355–63

A comparison with Malory shows how T shifts the blame for the
fall of Camelot on to the women. T's obsession with women and
their potential for evil can be traced throughout his work.
Miller offers an early and vigorous feminist critique which is
vehemently objected to by John Killham in 'Tennyson and the
Sinful Queen – A Corrected Impression', *NQ* 5 (1958) 507–11:
'To try to penetrate [T's] mask with tools as crude as Mrs.
Miller's is . . . unwittingly, of course . . . to play the part of
wilful defacer of works of art'.

355   Tennyson, Charles
'The *Idylls of the King*', *Twentieth Century* 161 (March 1957)
277–86

This considers the reasons for the postponement of T's
Arthurian project and gives an account of the various stages of
its production, acknowledging the influence of James Knowles
in encouraging the enterprise.

356   Miller, Betty
       'Camelot at Cambridge', *Twentieth Century* 163 (1958) 133–
       47

A provocative if not entirely convincing essay which argues that
Arthur Hallam and Cambridge were indeed the model for
Camelot but that the Apostles did not live up to expectations,
their own as well as those of others. *Idylls*, therefore, is not only
'an elegy for promise unfulfilled, or for aspiration quenched in
death, but, no less tragically, for high hopes cut short by life
itself, suffocated by the slow pressure of unproductive years'.

357   Madden, W. A.
       'The Burden of the Artist', 1859: ENTERING AN AGE OF
       CRISIS, ed. Philip Appleman, W. A. Madden and M. Wolff
       (Bloomington: Indiana UP, 1959)

This includes discussion of the first four *Idylls* as responses to
Darwin's *On the Origin of Species*.

358   Smalley, D.
       'A New Look at Tennyson – and Especially the *Idylls*', *JEGP*
       61 (1962) 349–57

Really a review of J. M. Buckley's *Tennyson* (121), this provides a useful survey of the critical estimation of *Idylls* from the
Victorian to the post-war period. Smalley notes that Buckley
resurrects *Idylls* from the obscurity that Nicolson had willingly
let fall upon them.

359   Litzinger, Boyd
       'The Structure of Tennyson's "The Last Tournament" ', *VP*
       1 (1963) 53–60

Litzinger argues that the success of this complex poem depends
on 'a remarkable unity of tone' deriving from the use of
recurrent images, the 'interweaving of parallel and antithetical
threads of narrative', and the skilful use of Dagonet, the fool.

360   Poston, Lawrence
        'The Argument of the Geraint-Enid Books in *Idylls of the King*', *VP* 2 (1964) 269–75

A decently argued essay on marital conflict and harmony and their relevance to *Idylls* as a whole.

361   Tillotson, Kathleen
        'Tennyson's Serial Poem', MID-VICTORIAN STUDIES, Geoffrey and Kathleen Tillotson (London: Athlone Press, 1965)

An important essay which discusses the growth of interest in the Arthurian legend during the nineteenth century and T's contribution to this. The writing of *Idylls of the King* 'took shape in sight of his readers. The process may fairly be called serial publication'. See also Roger Simpson, 'Costello's "The Funeral Boat": An Analogue of Tennyson's "The Lady of Shalott" ', *TRB* (1984) 129–31; and 'Landon's "A Legend of Tintagel Castle": Another Analogue of Tennyson's "The Lady of Shalott" ', *TRB* (1985) 179–85, where Simpson argues that the Arthurian legends were reasonably well known in the 1820s and 1830s.

362   Kozicki, Henry
        'Tennyson's *Idylls of the King* as Tragic Drama', *VP* 4 (1966) 15–20

Arthur is perceived as the Year Daemon whose rise and fall follows the seasons of the year. The pattern of history in *Idylls* is tragic, that of 'inevitable justice within the unknowable mystery'.

363   Poston, Lawrence
        ' "Pelleas and Ettarre": Tennyson's Troilus', *VP* 4 (1966) 199–204

A neatly argued essay on 'Pelleas and Ettarre' as a lesson on 'the perils of misguided idealism and submission to fortune'. Poston connects the poem to 'The Holy Grail' which explores 'the worthiness of men to perceive what is ideal'.

364   Ryals, Clyde de L.
       FROM THE GREAT DEEP: ESSAYS ON *IDYLLS OF
       THE KING* (Athens, Ohio: Ohio UP, 1967)

One of the most thoroughgoing 1960s attempts, which makes
use of essays by Ryals published elsewhere, to establish *Idylls* as
a philosophical work. Ryals argues that T is concerned with a
paradox centred on Arthur: that the heights of heroic expec-
tancy he embodies inevitably cause a cataclysmic fall in the
imperfect world of Camelot. Ryals's discussion is stimulating
(although sometimes given to specious philosophising) but
takes no account of the historical context in which the poems
were written, though he does concede that the later *Idylls* may
have been written in response to public reaction, and so that
their readers might 'readily see the relationship between the
poems and modern life'. Ryals is also selective in his discussion
of symbolism, a point made in a highly critical review by E. D.
H. Johnson, *VS* 12 (1968) 113–15.

365   Shaw, W. David
       'The Idealist's Dilemma in *Idylls of the King*', *VP* 5 (1967)
       41–53

Shaw argues that although all idealisms described in *Idylls* fail,
the mythic structures T employs endorse the poem's meaning,
which is that the struggle towards the ideal must always con-
tinue; this is the implication of Arthur's 'coming again'.

366   Reed, John R.
       PERCEPTION AND DESIGN IN TENNYSON'S *IDYLLS
       OF THE KING* (Athens, Ohio: Ohio UP, 1969)

T said, 'I think Matter more mysterious than Spirit. I can
conceive, in a way, what Spirit is, but not Matter'. Reed bases
his study on this Tennysonian belief that the material world is
inescapably ambiguous and only derives meaning from man's
moral perceptions. He traces a redemptive pattern in *Idylls*
from pride, through humbling, to love, but his argument is
somewhat vitiated by a reductive treatment of the poems to
make them fit the 'conversion' thesis.

367   Shaw, W. David
       '*Idylls of the King*: A Dialectical Reading', *VP* 7 (1969)
       175–90

       Shaw divides the sequence into four sets of complementary
       poems according to Hegelian dialectical principles of empiri-
       cism and idealism, scepticism and credulity, sexuality and
       repression, atheism and mysticism: Arthur's presence is de-
       signed to moderate between these extremes. Like many crit-
       icisms which impose a philosophical scheme on *Idylls*, this essay
       tends to simplify the poem. A similar argument is advanced by
       Henry Kozicki, 'A Dialectic of History in Tennyson's *Idylls*',
       VS 20 (1977) 141–57.

368   Goldfarb, Russell M.
       'Alfred Tennyson's "Lancelot and Elaine" and "Pelleas and
       Ettarre" ', SEXUAL REPRESSION AND VICTORIAN
       LITERATURE (Lewisburg, Pennsylvania: Bucknell UP,
       1970)

       A Freudian reading in which Lancelot's shield is Elaine's fetish
       and Pelleas, in discarding his sword, rejects sexuality and
       Camelot: a lively essay, perhaps rather simplistic.

369   Eggers, J. Philip
       KING ARTHUR'S LAUREATE: A STUDY OF
       TENNYSON'S *IDYLLS* (New York: New York UP, 1971)

       Eggers's point is that T used Arthur's order as a metaphor for
       Victorian idealism: 'The fall of the order is a warning to any
       contemporary idealists that the distance between Victorian
       England and Utopia is enormous'. On metaphors and imagery,
       Eggers's account is useful but he insufficiently documents the
       social conditions and aspirations for which Camelot is sup-
       posedly a metaphor.

370   Gray, J. M.
       'Tennyson's Doppelganger: "Balin and Balan" ', *TSM* No. 3
       (Lincoln: The Tennyson Society, 1971)

       This is a close analysis of the prosody and imagery of one of the
       more neglected of *Idylls*. Gray argues that 'Balin and Balan'
       should be read as a psychodrama which reveals an intense

interest in the motivation and construction of character; all the figures encountered by Balin are elements of his own mind.

371   McCullough, Joseph B. and Brew, Claude C.
'A Study of the Publication of Tennyson's *Idylls of the King*', *Papers of the Bibliographical Society of America* 65 (1971) 156–69

On the editions of *Idylls* published during T's lifetime.

372   Hunt, J. Dixon
'The Poetry of Distance: Tennyson's *Idylls of the King*', VICTORIAN POETRY, ed. Malcolm Bradbury and David Palmer (London: Edward Arnold; New York: Crane, Russak (Stratford upon Avon Studies, 15), 1972) 89–121

Hunt notes that T dwells throughout *Idylls* on 'possibilities of distance, pictures and the past', a preoccupation which Arthur Hallam had noted. By this long focus, which Hunt compares to techniques in Pre-Raphaelite art, T sought to make the past relevant to the present; at his best T maintains an imaginative distance against what Yeats called 'a pushing world'. This is a cogently argued and well-illustrated essay.

373   Pfordresher, John
'A Bibliographical History of Alfred Tennyson's *Idylls of the King*', *SB* 26 (1973) 193–218

This lists the manuscripts and proofs and also discusses the composition of the poem.

374   Rosenberg, John D.
THE FALL OF CAMELOT (Cambridge, Mass.: HUP, 1973)

Rosenberg sees T as a precursor of the French *symboliste* poets, one who 'creates an inclusive psychological landscape in which all the separate consciousnesses in the poem participate and in which each action is bound to all others through symbol, prophecy or retrospect'. Rosenberg's 'synoptic perspective' aims to reveal the complex unity of a poem in which 'character cannot be abstracted from symbol and both have no substance apart from the narrative in which they are embedded'. A sophisticated and revealing study.

375   Kozicki, Henry
        'Wave and Fire Imagery in Tennyson's *Idylls of the King*', *VN* 43 (1973) 21–3

        A closely argued essay which suggests that T's apparently inconsistent use of this imagery is explicable in the context of his view of history as cyclic.

376   McSweeney, Kerry
        'Tennyson's Quarrel with Himself: The Tristram Group of *Idylls*, *VP* 15 (1977) 49–59

        This argues that the Tristram group – 'Balin and Balan', 'Pelleas and Ettarre' and 'The Last Tournament' – are Orphic and erotic, unlike the predominantly philosophical remainder of the sequence. McSweeney provides an intelligent counter to the view that *Idylls* is morally and/or philosophically homogeneous.

377   Homans, Margaret
        'Tennyson and the Spaces of Life', *ELH* 46 (1979) 693–709

        A complex and clever article, influenced by Harold Bloom's *The Anxiety of Influence* (1973), which reads *Idylls* as the attempt by a 'weak' poet to literalise what had been figurative in the poetry of his 'strong' precursor, Wordsworth.

378   Gray, J. M.
        THRO' THE VISION OF THE NIGHT (Edinburgh: Edinburgh UP; Montreal: McGill-Queens, 1980)

        '. . . not a critical judgement of the *Idylls* [but] an enquiry into the *poetic process* [which] involves close *explication* and *analysis* of the texts'. Describes the serial evolution of *Idylls*, densely documents its relationship to literary predecessors, particularly Malory's *Le Morte D'Arthur*; defends its descriptiveness, verbal ingenuities and archaisms and its characterisation; notes its many cross-references and other compositional features. Gray's book is leaden but necessary reading for serious students of the *Idylls*.

379   Stevenson, Catherine B.
'How It Struck a Contemporary: Tennyson's "Lancelot and Elaine" and Pre-Raphael Art', *VN* 60 (1981) 8–14

T was alert to the artistic issues raised by the Pre-Raphaelites, particularly with regard to the 1857 Moxon edition. The figure of Elaine 'embodies Tennyson's thoughts on Pre-Raphaelitism and the problem of integrating the literal/empirical with the visionary/imaginative'.

380   Fertel, Randy J.
'Anti-Pastoral and the Attack on Naturalism in Tennyson's *Idylls of the King*', *VP* 19 (1981) 337–50

Fertel's suggestion is that pastoral sentiments in *Idylls* are perceived as false and where indulged in, as in Tristram's case, can only lead to brutishness. T shared with Carlyle, Mill and Arnold the belief that 'we can love nature only by helping it to move upward'.

381   Staines, David
TENNYSON'S CAMELOT: THE *IDYLLS OF THE KING* AND ITS MEDIEVAL SOURCES (Waterloo, Ontario: Wilfred Laurier UP, 1982)

Staines's purpose is to study the way T shaped his source material to create his own Camelot with the central character being Guinevere, whom T develops considerably from Malory's shadowy figure. Not particularly illuminating as criticism, this book is a useful collation of information on sources and parallels and includes an interesting epilogue on 'Alfred Tennyson and Victorian Arthuriana' which discusses T's influence on Rossetti and other Pre-Raphaelites, and on Swinburne and Morris.

382   Culver, Marcia C.
'The Death and Birth of an Epic: Tennyson's "Morte d'Arthur" ', *VP* 20 (1982) 51–61

A clear and careful account, using the available manuscripts, of the various stages in T's treatment of the death of Arthur – from the first bleak attempts at 'Morte d'Arthur' in the early 1830s to the more hopeful framing of the poem by 'The Epic' in 1842, which prepares the way for the philosophical treatment of the theme in *Idylls*.

383   Kiernan, Victor
        'Tennyson, King Arthur and Imperialism', CULTURE,
        IDEOLOGY AND POLITICS, ed. Raphael Samuel and
        Gareth Stedman (London: Routledge & Kegan Paul, 1983)

        The Crimean War and the Indian Mutiny were the background
        to the first group of *Idylls* and in this context the poems can be
        read as imperialist with a paternalistic Arthur creating 'an
        aristocracy of merit'.

384   Sparer, D. J.
        'Arthur's Vast Design', *VP* 21 (1983) 119–31

        A convincingly argued case for the 'objective reality' of Cam-
        elot in Arthur's moral design. Camelot reveals Arthur's pur-
        poses more clearly than other elements in the poem; in
        particular, its absence of militarism and the predominance of
        female figures and attributes indicate Arthur's attempts to
        create a more virtuous society and more civilised notions of
        manhood.

385   Gilbert, Elliot L.
        'The Female King: Tennyson's Arthurian Apocalypse',
        PMLA 98 (1983) 863–78

        One of the best modern essays on the question of Arthur's
        effeminacy. Gilbert shows how T's interpretation of the
        Arthurian myth challenges patriarchal concepts; Arthur rules
        without patrilineal authority and takes his power from women
        and from nature. But if history and legitimacy are denied, so is
        succession, and the rampant ahistorical power of female sex-
        uality destroys Camelot, just as it was popularly believed that
        the power of female lust was responsible for the bloody end of
        another illegitimate reign, that which held place during the
        French Revolution.

386   Lang, Cecil Y.
        'Tennyson's Arthurian Psycho-Drama', *TSOP* 5 (Lincoln:
        The Tennyson Society, 1983)

        The text of an address to the Tennyson Society, this is a clever and amusing discussion of the importance to T in his conception of King Arthur of both Arthur Hallam and Arthur Wellesley (Duke of Wellington): 'the real subject of this great poem is the British Empire'. Lang also speculates on the presence in *Idylls* of various other personalities T knew, such as his sons Hallam and Lionel as Balin and Balan.

387 Knight, Stephen
' "The Phantom King": Tennyson's Arthurian *Idylls*',
ARTHURIAN LITERATURE AND SOCIETY (London: Macmillan, 1983) 149–86

This is Chapter 5 of a study of Arthurian writing from the earliest Welsh versions to Mark Twain and other modern 'legends'. Knight's opinion is that for T Arthur is 'a sort of ghost, a "phantom king" in reality, because he was a figure of ideology created to grapple with issues without revealing their full nature . . . The true concern of [*Idylls*] was to defend the patriarchal family and the conservative state'.

388 Buckler, William E.
MAN AND HIS MYTHS: TENNYSON'S *IDYLLS OF THE KING* IN CRITICAL CONTEXT (New York and London: New York UP, 1984)

Some solemn exegesis here, plus what the author describes as 'a judicious representation of the ways in which other commentators have perceived [*Idylls*] over the last thirty years'. Buckler gives the impression that *Idylls* has attracted some of the most boring and ponderous criticism ever written on a major poem.

Other individual poems

389 Haight, Gordon S.
'Tennyson's Merlin', *Studies in Philology* 44 (1947) 549–66

Discusses 'Merlin and the Gleam' as an autobiographical poem. For a recent account of the poem, see Linda K. Hughes, 'Text and Subtext in "Merlin and the Gleam" ', *VP* 23 (1985) 161–9.

390   Stange, G. Robert
       'Tennyson's Mythology: A Study of "Demeter and
       Persephone" ', *ELH* 21 (1954) 67–80, in Killham (122)

       An interesting article which defines myth as 'a figurative expres-
       sion of personal concerns' and compares T's use of it with that
       of G. S. Fraser in *The Golden Bough*, particularly in its
       application to the radical dualities of human experience.

391   Robson, W.W.
       'The Dilemma of Tennyson', *Listener* 57 (June 1957) 963–5,
       in Killham (122)

       Concludes with an attack on 'Locksley Hall Sixty Years After'
       as a symptom of 'the breakdown of relation between Ten-
       nyson's "art" and his "social conscience" '.

392   Kincaid, James R.
       'Tennyson's "Crossing the Bar": A Poem of Frustration', *VP*
       3 (1965) 57–61

       By means of a detailed technical analysis of metre and imagery,
       Kincaid suggestively argues that 'beneath the placid surface of
       the poem . . . runs a dark current of frustration'.

393   Tennyson, Sir Charles
       'Tennyson's "Doubt and Prayer" Sonnet', *VP* 6 (1968) 1–3

       Sir Charles reproduces the manuscript (in Hallam Tennyson's
       hand, revised by T) of 'The Xtian Penitent An Early Sonnet',
       finally published as 'Doubt and Prayer' in 1892.

394   Scott, P. G.
       'Tennyson's *Enoch Arden*: A Victorian Best-Seller' *TSM* No.
       2 (Lincoln: The Tennyson Society, 1970)

       An interesting study divided into four sections: the breadth of
       'Enoch Arden''s readership; why T chose the subject; the
       poem's contemporary critical reception; elements the poem has
       in common with popular Victorian narrative. There is also a
       note on film versions.

395 Sonstroem, David
' "Crossing the Bar" as Last Word', *VP* 8 (1970) 55–60

This lists the criticism to date of the poem that T requested should be placed last in collections of his poetry. Sonstroem contributes the opinion that in the light of T's other poems this poem can be seen as a summary and resolution of 'a divided poet's struggle to compose himself'.

396 Drake, Constance
'A Topical Dating for "Locksley Hall Sixty Years After" ', *VP* 10 (1972) 307–20

By concentrating on the topical issues raised in this poem, Drake convincingly argues that it was composed earlier than Hallam Tennyson's suggested date in *Memoir* of 1886.

397 Shaw, W. David
'Imagination and Intellect in Tennyson's "Lucretius" ', MLQ 33 (1972) 130–9

Lucretius's monologue is characterised by a 'dissociation of sensibility'; he represents a search for a synthesis of facts and values in a post-Romantic culture.

398 Adler, Joshua
'Tennyson's "Mother of Sorrows": "Rizpah" ', *VP* 12 (1974) 363–9

The powerful effect of this poem is due to the fusion of a sympathetic depiction of abnormal mental states and a skilful use of biblical associations.

399 Fricke, Douglas C.
'A Study of Myth and Archetype in "Enoch Arden" ', *TRB* (1974) 106–15

A mythic pattern, of the type Maud Bodkin describes as the Paradise–Hades archetype, structures 'Enoch Arden' in which the hero follows a cyclic, life–death–rebirth journey: an interesting article which goes some way to explain the dissonances of style and subject matter in the poem.

400   Libera, Sharon Mayer
        'John Tyndall and Tennyson's "Lucretius" ', *VN* 45 (Spring
        1974) 19–22

        The physicist Tyndall was the leading exponent of the Lucretian
        concept of an atomistic universe. T called on Tyndall in Decem-
        ber 1985 during his composition of 'Lucretius' and their discus-
        sions influenced the poem, though T's conclusion was that
        classical materialism was an inadequate explanation of life.

401   Shaw, W David
        'Tennyson's Late Elegies', *VP* 12 (1974) 1–12

        'In the Garden at Swainston' (1870), 'To the Marquis of
        Dufferin and Avon' (1889), and 'Crossing the Bar' (1889)
        display austerities of style and thought reminiscent of 'Break,
        Break, Break' and parts of *In Memoriam*. These 'desperately
        impoverished poems' are in contrast to the richness of T's
        classical elegies, 'Frater Ave Atque Vale' and 'To Virgil'.

402   Wilkenfeld, Roger B.
        ' "Columbus" and "Ulysses": Notes on the Development of
        a Tennysonian Theme', *VP* 12 (1974) 170–4

        The 'need for going forward and braving the struggles of life' in
        'Ulysses' is reworked in 'a minor, more introspective key in
        "Columbus" (1880)'.

403   Whitbread, L. G.
        'Tennyson's "In the Garden at Swainston" ', *VP* 13 (1975)
        61–9

        A detailed discussion of the allusions in this poem and of the
        life, family and talents of Sir John Simeon, whose death it
        occasioned.

404   Goslee, David F.
        'Three Stages of Tennyson's "Tiresias" ', *JEGP* 75 (1976)
        154–67

        This traces the development of the poem from eight lines
        written before Hallam's death, through seventy-five lines writ-

ten just after Hallam's death, to the concluded and revised version of 1883. T's evolving attitudes to this mythic character represent resignation to losses within his own life: that of innocence, of Hallam, and of reputation in old age.

405   Durham, Margery Stricker
       'Tennyson's Wellington Ode and the Cosmology of Love',
       VP 14 (1976) 277–92

Durham regards the Ode as a 'sensitive, flawed but honest attempt to make an effective ritual' by which the sense of community may be renewed and the principle of providential purpose recognised.

406   Francis, Elizabeth A.
       'Tennyson's Political Poetry, 1852–1855', *VP* 14 (1976) 113–23

The intense and apocalyptic language of these anonymously published poems partook of the bellicose rhetoric of the times, but it was also a long-standing feature of T's verse dating from *Poems by Two Brothers* and brought to a controlled climax in *Maud*.

407   Hughes, Linda K.
       'Tennyson's "Columbus": "Sense at War with Soul" Again',
       VP 15 (1977) 171–6

Considers the poem in the context of the ageing T's despair around the period of writing this poem and sees it as a prototype of late monologues such as 'The Ancient Sage' and 'Akbar's Dream'.

408   Gates, Barbara
       'Victorian Attitudes Toward Suicide and Mr. Tennyson's "Despair" ', *TRB* (1979) 101–9

T's 'dark dramatic monologue', 'Despair' (1881), met with a hostile reception, including Swinburne's parody 'Disgust'. Gates's argument is that this reaction was excessive and had much to do with contemporary sensitivity and controversy concerning 'the right to die'.

409   McGann, Jerome J.
        'Tennyson and the History of Criticism', *Review* 4 (1982)
        219–53

        Ostensibly a review of recent books on T, this becomes an
        account of 'The Charge of the Light Brigade' and the various
        critical responses there have been to it. McGann's firm convic-
        tion is that the significance and achievement of the poem can
        emerge only through a critical elucidation of its historical
        aspects. McGann also notes the eclectic nature of the poem: for
        example, images are drawn from popular newspaper reports
        but the form of the poem is traditional and heroic.

410   Fulweiler, Howard W.
        'The Argument of "The Ancient Sage": Tennyson and the
        Christian Intellectual Tradition', *VP* 21 (1983) 203–16

        This argues that 'The Ancient Sage' mediates thoughtfully
        between the intellectual tradition represented by Plato and St
        Augustine and the Christian Romanticism of Coleridge and
        Wordsworth.

411   Alexander, Michael
        'Tennyson's "The Battle of Brunanburh" ', *TRB* (1985)
        151–61

        T considered this battle the most heroic and patriotic of battles
        and esteemed the Old English poem, his version of which he
        published in 1880 among his Translations.

The Plays

Tennyson wrote seven plays; this is to exclude the boyhood composition *The Devil and the Lady* which is usually classified with his juvenilia in poetry and which was not published during his lifetime.

The plays were published as follows:

1875 *Queen Mary*
1876 ('1877') *Harold*
1882 *The Promise of May*
1884 *The Cup*
  The Falcon
  Becket
1892 *The Foresters*

Queen Mary was first produced in 1876, *The Falcon* in 1879, *The Cup* in 1881, *The Promise of May* in 1882 and *The Foresters* in 1892. *Harold* was not produced during the nineteenth century.

The plays are printed in the Eversley edition (85) of *The Works of Lord Tennyson Annotated* and in the Oxford Standard Authors edition (89).

412   Waugh, Arthur
       ALFRED, LORD TENNYSON: A STUDY OF THE LIFE
       AND WORK (London: Heinemann, 1892) 213–70

       This contains one of the fullest accounts of the dramas and is interesting in being a near-contemporary summary of their overall critical reception. Waugh is sympathetic towards the endeavour and thinks that the plays contain many good things but they are unwieldy and lack stagecraft.

413   James, Henry
       'Tennyson's Drama', VIEWS AND REVIEWS (Boston, Mass.: The Ball Publishing Co., 1908; reprinted 1968) 165–204

       Originally reviews of *Queen Mary* and *Harold* in 1875 and 1877 respectively, this essay states that T had 'not so much refuted as evaded the charge that he is not a dramatic poet' since the plays bear no trace of his characteristic talents. *Queen Mary* has an elevated tone but no subject worth speaking of and *Harold* is a 'graceless anomaly'. James also registers the decline in T's general reputation at this time, describing him as a poet 'whom one thinks most of while one's taste is immature'.

414   Granville-Barker, Harley
'Tennyson, Swinburne, Meredith – and the Theatre', THE EIGHTEEN-SEVENTIES: ESSAYS BY FELLOWS OF THE ROYAL SOCIETY OF LITERATURE, ed. H. Granville-Barker (Cambridge: CUP, 1929) 161–91

Granville-Barker despairs generally of the dramas attempted by poets at this time and thinks T particularly mistaken in attempting to revive Elizabethan dramatic forms.

415   Baum, Paull F.
'Poet as Playwright', TENNYSON SIXTY YEARS AFTER (N. Carolina: N. Carolina UP, 1948) 214–19

Considers T took 'a brave step in the wrong direction'.

416   Irving, Lawrence
HENRY IRVING: THE ACTOR AND HIS WORLD (London: Faber & Faber, 1951)

This contains accounts of T's troubled association with Irving, whom T had in mind to play the major parts in and produce several of his plays. Irving adapted *Queen Mary* and *Becket* for the stage. See particularly pp. 264–75 and 554–62.

417   Eidson, John Olin
'The Reception of Tennyson's Plays in America', *PQ* 35 (1956) 435–43

Eidson shows that American criticism was harsh but not so severe as the British. There was amazement at T venturing into drama and an inevitable, and unfavourable, comparison with Shakespeare. *The Promise of May* (a prose play) was the least well received.

418   Buckley, Jerome H.
'Under the Mask: The Plays, 1875–1882', TENNYSON:
THE GROWTH OF A POET (Cambridge, Mass.: HUP,
1960) 195–215

A sympathetic account of T's venture into drama, particularly
of the painstakingly researched and written *Queen Mary*:
'Whatever his inexperience and naivete as dramatist, he suc-
ceeded admirably in suggesting the temper of an age . . . Apart
from its faithfulness as a historical record, which mitigates its
power as a play, the strength of *Queen Mary* lies in its able
characterization'.

419   Richardson, Joanna
'Laureate and Lyceum' and 'Plays and Tragedies', THE
PRE-EMINENT VICTORIAN. A STUDY OF
TENNYSON (Westport, Connecticut: Greenwood Press,
1962) 198–204, 213–18

Two chapters in Richardson's readable biography which place
the writing and productions of T's plays in the context of his late
Laureateship.

420   Knight, G. Wilson
'Victorian', THE GOLDEN LABYRINTH: A STUDY OF
BRITISH DRAMA (London: Phoenix House, 1962)

This contains a few pages (262–8) on T's patriot dramas (*Queen
Mary*, *Harold* and *Becket*) in which Knight believes T to have
been 'looking for origins, asking how Great Britain came to
greatness'.

421   Rehak, Louise Rouse
'On the Use of Martyrs: Tennyson and Eliot on Thomas
Becket', *UTQ* 33 (1963–4) 43–60

An interesting comparison which argues that T's 'humanist'
play deals with the 'real universals of human nature' and Eliot's
with the 'concepts of a limited theology'. Rehak concludes that
T's human sympathies are wider than Eliot's but his theatrical
sense is less well developed.

422 Solimine, Joseph
'The Dialectics of Church and State: Tennyson's Historical Plays', *The Personalist* XLVII (1966) 218–25

On *Becket* and *Harold* as demonstrations of T's belief in the need for the spiritual and the secular to be interrelated, and of his distrust, in *Harold* particularly, of asceticism.

423 Otten, T. J.
'Tennyson's *Maud* and *Becket*', THE DESERTED STAGE: THE SEARCH FOR DRAMATIC FORM IN NINETEENTH CENTURY ENGLAND (Athens, Ohio: Ohio UP, 1972) 76–107

Otten argues that T's plays were a failure because he pursued a dying dramatic tradition. The subjectivism of *Maud* and its experimentalism of form demonstrate 'the outlines of a new drama' which, however, T was unable to develop because he 'could not envision in the 1850s a stage capable of producing *Maud*'. He could not 'bridge the gap between writing a drama situated in plot and a drama rooted in character'.

424 Thomson, Peter
'Tennyson's Plays and Their Production', in Palmer (125) 226–54

This evaluates the plays as dramatic literature and summarises the history of their performances.

425 Grosskurth, Phyllis
'Tennyson, Froude, and *Queen Mary*', *TRB* (1973) 44–54

An interesting article on T's debt to Vol. VI of Froude's *History of England* and the cautious revisions that were made to the play before performance to soften its anti-Catholicism.

426 Sait, James E.
'Tennyson's *The Princess* and *Queen Mary*: Two Examinations of Sex and Politics', *Durham University Journal* 37 (1975) 70–8

The Princess optimistically and *Queen Mary* pessimistically explore familial and sexual roles within a political context to affirm T's views of 'civilisation's necessities' as the 'proper dispensation of feminine and masculine character traits, interaction between men and women, and generation'.

Subject Index

References are to entry numbers

Index of Authors, Editors and Others Cited

References are to entry numbers

Index of Poems and Plays

References are to entry numbers